THE

MUSIC-LESSON OF CONFUCIUS,

AND OTHER POEMS.

THE MUSIC-LESSON OF CONFUCIUS,

And Other Poems.

BY

CHARLES GODFREY LELAND.

BOSTON:
JAMES R. OSGOOD AND COMPANY,
LATE TICKNOR AND FIELDS, AND FIELDS, OSGOOD, AND CO.
1872.

CONTENTS.

THE MUSIC-LESSON OF CONFUCIUS.

THE music-lesson of Koung-tseu the wise,
Known as Confucius in the western world.

Of all the sages of the Flowery Land
None knew so well as great Confucius
The ancient rites; and when his mother died,
Three years he mourned alone beside her tomb
As the Old Custom bade, nor did he miss
A single detail of the dark old forms
Required of the bereaved, for he had made
Himself a model for all living men:
A mirror and a pattern of the Past.

Now when the years of mourning with their rites
Were at an end, Confucius came forth
And wandered as of old with other men,
Giving his counsel unto many kings;
But still the hand of grief was on his heart,
And his dark hue set forth his darkened hours.
To drive away these sorrows from his soul,
Remembering that music had been made
A moral motive in the golden books
Of wisdom by the sacred ancestors,
He played upon the Kin—the curious lute
Invented by Fou-Hi in days of old;

Fou-Hi of the bull's head and dragon's form,
The Lord of Learning who upraised mankind
From being silent brutes to singing men.

In vain Confucius played upon the lute;
He found that music would not be to him
What it had been of old—a pastime gay:
For he had borne through three long years of grief
Stupendous knowledge, and his mighty soul,
Grasping the lines which link all earthly lore,
Had been by suffering raised to greater power:
For he who *knows* and suffers, if he will
May raise himself unnumbered scales o'er man.

The music spoke no more its wonted sounds,
But whispered mysteries in a broken tongue
Which urged him sorely. Then Confucius said:
'O secret Music! sacred tongue of God!
I hear thee calling to me, and I come!
Of old I did but know thy outer form
And dreamed not of the spirit hid within;
The Goddess in the Lotus. Yes, I come,
And will not rest—nor will I calm my doubt
Till I have seen thee plainly with mine eyes,
And palpably have touched thee with my hand,
Then shall I know thee—raised to life for me
For what thou truly art.
Lo! I have heard
That in the land of Kin a master lives,
So deeply skilled in music, that mankind
Begin again to give a glowing faith
Unto the golden stories which are told
Of the strange harmonies which built the world,
And of the melody whose key is God.
Now I will travel to the land of Kin,
And know this sage of music, great Siang,

And learn the secret lore which hides within
All sweet well-ordered sounds.' He went his way,
Nor rested till he stood before the man.

Thus spoke Siang unto Confucius:
'Of all the arts, great Music is the art
To raise the soul above all earthly storms;
For in it lies that *purest harmony*
Which lifts us over self and up to God.
Thou who hast studied deeply the *Kouà*—
The eight great symbols of created things—
Knowest the sacred power of the line
Which when unbroken flies to all the worlds
As light unending—but in broken forms
Falls short as sky and earth, clouds, winds, and fire,
The deep blue ocean and the mountain high,
And the red lightning hissing in the wave.
The mighty law which formed what thou canst see,
As clearly lives in all that thou canst hear,
And more than this, in all that thou canst feel.
Here, take thy lute in hand. I teach the air
Made by the sage Wen Wang of ancient days.'

Confucius took the lute and played the air
Till all his soul seemed passing into song;
Then he fell deep into the solemn chords
As though his body and the lute were one,
And every chord a wave which bore him on
Through the great sea of ecstasy. His hands
Then ceased to play—but in his raptured look
They saw him following out the harmony.

Five days went by, and still Confucius
Played all day long the ancient simple air;
And when Siang would teach him more, he said:
'Not yet, my master, I would seize the *thought*,

The subtle thought which hides within the tune.'
To which the master answered: 'It is well.
Take five days more!' And when the time was passed
Unto Siang thus spoke Confucius:
'I do begin to see—yet what I see
Is very dim. I am as one who looks
And nothing sees except a luminous cloud:
Give me but five more days, and at the end
If I have not attained the great idea
Hidden of old within the melody,
I will leave music as beyond my power.'
'Do as thou wilt, Oh pupil!' cried Siang
In deepest admiration; 'never yet
Had I a scholar who was like to thee.'

And on the fifteenth day Confucius rose
And stood before Siang, and cried aloud:
'The mist which shadowed me is blown away,
I am as one who stands upon a cliff
And gazes far and wide upon the world,
For I have mastered every secret thought,
Yea, every shadow of a feeling dim
Which flitted through the spirit of Wen Wang
When he composed that air. I speak to him,
I hear him clearly answer me again;
And more than that—I see his very form:
A man of middle stature, with a hue
Half blended with the dark and with the fair;
His features long—and large sweet eyes which beam
With great benevolence—a noble face!
His voice is deep and full, and all his air
Inspires a sense of virtue and of love.
I know that I behold the very man,
The sage of ancient days, Wen Wang the just.'

Then good Siang lay down upon the dust,
And said : 'Thou art my master. Even thus
The ancient legend, known to none but me,
Describes our first great sire. And thou hast seen
That which I never yet myself beheld,
Though I have played the sacred song for years,
Striving with all my soul to penetrate
Its mystery unto the master's form,
Whilst thou hast reached it at a single bound :—
Henceforth the gods alone can teach thee tune.'

THE RETURN OF THE GODS.

'Greece so thoroughly wrought out its conception of the beautiful human animal as to make an idol of it, and in order to glorify it on earth they made a divinity of it in heaven.'—*The Philosophy of Art, by H. Taine.*

LIKE one who looks over a city when day is beginning
to break,
I look o'er the million-homed age where we live, in the
dusk of the dawn,
Seeing the sunlight on steeples, or edging the turrets
and towers,
While the streets and the low-lying houses are grey in
the gloaming or gloom.
Light in the eye of the thinker ; light on the brow of
the wise,
Dimmering shade in the spirit of him who is hopeless
and low.

But far on the fire-flashing mountains which circle the
town of the time
Flame brighter and higher the glories, though deeper
and grander the gloom.
Like gods freshly set on the summits, just resting a
moment, but soon

To sweep down the sides to the valleys, and conquer
the giants of night.
Yes, they are coming in glory again to resplendour the
world,
The gods whom we thought were long-perished:
Olympus is coming again.

In the roar of the terrible engine, in boats which go
onward by steam,
Or the pathways of iron extending from ocean to
ocean unbent,
In bridges once buried, deep hidden, now binding the
summits of cliffs;
In wheels which are whirling for ever to multiply
comfort for man:
All this but the little beginning—all this but the
mustard-seed small;
When all is unfolded, oh Vulcan, wilt thou not be with
us again?

When Genius in infinite channels, when Labour with
infinite might
Shall have solved all the problems we dream of, while
solving, creating anew;
When the branches while further diverging send
quicker the sap to the root
And the highest adventurous blossom feels deepest its
part in the whole,
Will Man then believe in his power, and, scorning the
petty and vile,
Be grand in his power creative and Vulcan be with us
again?

Phul Khan—Tubal Cain—the Fire Monarch—first
king and first master of Iron!
They could not dispense with the blacksmith, the
smith who by right was a god

And the right-hand of every warrior, yes, even the master of Mars;
But they shamed him and lamed him, those proud ones, and punished him with his reward.
Now he cometh, he cometh in glory, his lameness and shame are removed,
And Art in its union with Beauty shines brighter with Honour and Pride.

Venus, the life of the lovely—soul of the exquisite charm!
Thou hast done penance for ages, as we thy poor children have done.
Short was the carnival season in the gay god-land of Greece,
Few were the guests at the banquet,—brief was the life of the flowers,
Long was the Lent which came after,—bitter the wailing and woe;—
But the trial was good for the mourners,—it humbled the cruel and proud,
It raised up the humble and fallen,—gave spirit and strength to the poor,
And is freeing from slavery Woman,—the slave of all ages gone by.

Enough of the sackcloth and ashes,—enough of the penance and pain,
Enough of deep woe for the Many and feverish joy for the Few;
Joy which defeats its own wishes and struggles in hard narrow rounds
Ignoring the truth that great Pleasure demands the great concourse of All.
Oh, Mother of rapture and Beauty—thou too hast done penance in grief,

Thou did'st rise from the Ocean in glory, red glowing
to kiss the warm sun !
Short were the luscious embraces—cold blew the wind
from the North,
Thou fell'st in sad tears from Heaven, and on earth
wert a torrent of tears.

Now in comfort, with justice and beauty and freedom
for woman and man,
Thou wilt rise in a rosier glory, and light every soul
with a ray.
For when Man shall have learned that the spirit of Sin
is but trespass and pain,
Trespass and pain on his fellow, or idle neglect of his
own,
And that Pleasure which injures none other and
wounds not the spirit of truth,
Has nothing in common with Evil and touches none
other but Self,
Then thou wilt be with us, sweet Mother, and charm
every soul with thy smile,
Raising to Art all our labour—and Love be the life of
the world.

Mars, the magnificent master of warfare with foes to
the gods,
Brilliant and bold and unbending thou too wilt rise on
with the rest,
For the progress of Man is the progress of gods in the
infinite scale,
He who lifts up the spear to do battle lifts also the
pennon and steel.
And though the point shine in the sunlight or gleam
in the glory of war,
Far over the head of the knight, it must wait till the
wood has been raised.

While Man is deep buried in valleys his gods live on
mountains above,
When he reaches the silvery summits they dwell in the
gold of the sky.

No more the Messiah of Murder will Mars be the
terror of Man,
No longer the dread of the lowly, the bravo exulting
in blood.
For in the great Fight of the Future our foes will be
mightier far
Than men of mere sinew and muscle,—those foes
which lie silent around ;—
The rugged rock-giants denying the room for existence
to all,
The awful deep Dragon of Ocean still keeping in
secret its plains,
And the solemn blue space yet unconquered which
parts us from numberless stars,
And the Fire-Land which burns in our centre,—these
foes still await thee, oh Mars !

For the doctor who drives out diseases or shortens the
power of death,
And the teacher who quickens the spirit and conquers
the darkness of crime,
The poet who blesses with beauty the soul which was
gloomy and grey,
The builder, the chemist, the workman, are warriors
each in their way :
For what were the Jotuns and Titans o'erwhelmed by
the gods of the Past
But the forces of fire and of mountains,—the giants we
are fighting to-day ?
Fighting more bravely than ever—fighting with better
success :—

Oh Mars, thou wert in the first battle—in the victory
be by our side!

I know that the swift-footed Hermes will soon be beloved again,
For already Man finds with strange rapture he holds
more than Mercury's power,
More than the might which was fabled to be that of
Hermes of old,
When he touches the telegraph deftly and talks over
oceans afar,
As we go faster in motion; faster in thought and in
speech,
Quicker in means of conveying and shortening the
path of ideas
Life will be lengthened while growing, for Thought is
the measure of life:
He who speaks or does most in a little is Mercury's
son and himself.

And with Labour and Love and with Conquest and
Speed all the rest will be won,
With Vulcan and Venus, and Ares, and Hermes fast
darting afar:
For Apollo with Muses and Graces—the exquisite
children of Art—
And the sense of the Lovely in Nature as shown in a
myriad gods,
All these are just hovering round us, awaiting a place
in our hearts,
Not as wearied-out forms of a worship which faded
long ages ago,
But as the fresh life of *all* worship, renewed in Man's
faith in himself:
The Man who has risen to Greatness was never yet
wanting in gods.

Do your hearts enter into my meaning, ye thinkers
who list to my song?
Do you feel that we come to *religion* in quitting the
vulgar and mean?
And that Man when he lives in the glory of conquest
and knows he is great
Soon learns that the power of crushing the Time-worn
means this—*to be free*,
Freedom with power creative, Greatness with Beauty
and Love,
Was, is, and shall be for ever, the Godlike in spirit and
truth.
And be it in smoke upon Sinai, in temples and
statues in Greece,
Or walking by Galilee's waters, the *noble* is ever a
god.

Grander than Plato or Hegel, greater than Bacon or
Comte,
Is faith in a noble endeavour, the power to rise to the
New:
And the scorn of the ancient Egyptian; of Hermes,
for those who but live
For idle *self-will* and dull pleasure—the million who
nothing create,
In the downward-born elements whirling away from
the centre of God—
Is the first of the wonderful chapter, long written and
yet to be writ,
Which told and will tell how the dawning drove
darkness away from the world,
And how the small sneer of the Devil was lost in
God's infinite smile.

This is the coming of Zeus—of Jove, the imperial
lord!

And of Juno his wife and his sister—the greatest are
ever akin—
That Man shall find out he is noble—this knowing he
finds out a god
And the glory of God will be with him when dignity
blesses his life.
Esculapius teaches the lesson—the purest of blood are
most free,
In strains without taint of disorder the nearest come
ever more near:
The souls which live Jove-like in calmness progress in
perfecting their type;
What Satan and folly have hidden, will rise in the
ages to come.

'How shall we see the Immortals, and when shall we
know they are come?
In Greece we beheld them in statues—unmoving im-
mortals in stone:
Closed in a book in Judea—frozen and centred in
One,
Blooming again into Many which flowed from the
mythical Three,
And burst into wide-flashing rainbows of colour and
legend and song
When the wonderful age mediæval threw pictures all
over the world?—'
Not in statues or books or in pictures, or churches or
legends or song
Will ye see the great gods of your worship whose
footsteps are sounding afar.

Ah no;—in yourselves will ye see them, when Venus
shall favour your love,
And man, fitly mated with woman, believes that his
love is divine:

When Passion shall elevate Woman to something so holy and grand,
That she—the ideal enraptured—shall ne'er be a check upon Man,
Then the children they bear will be holy, and Beauty shall make them her own,
And Man in the eyes of his neighbour will gaze on the reflex divine
Of the God he inclines to in spirit—or trace in each feature and limb
The lines which the body inherits from souls which are noble and true.

Would thou could'st feel in deep earnest, how beautiful God will be then,
When we see him as Jove or Apollo in men who inspire us with love,
As Juno and Venus the holy, in women who know not the mean,
And feel not the influence cruel of hardness and self-love and scorn.
Would thou could'st once know how real the presence of God will become,
How earnest and ever more earnest thy faith when thyself shall be great,
And from the true worship of others thou'lt learn what is holy in them,
And rise to the infinite fountain of glory which flows in us all.

But when shall we see the Immortals?—believe me —whenever ye will
They are near us, around us, within us, awaiting our wish and our word.
More than thy dreams ever pictured, more than thy heart ever dreamed,

Will pour in increasing abundance on him who has
freedom and faith ;
Freedom from meanness and harshness—faith in the
Godhood within—
The ore lies before us in mountains—we've power to
change it to gold :—
Be to thyself what thou lovest, and others will be unto
thee
What thou wilt. When in God thou believest near
God thou wilt certainly be !

ON MOUNT MERU.

Will the time come when man, the all-conquering, shall lay his hand on the past as on a weapon and say, with it in his terrible grasp, to the future, 'Be thou my slave'?

IN earliest ages on Mount Meru
Stood together and talked, the Two.

Gazing far from the golden berg,
The Dæmon spoke to the Demiurg.

'All is beautiful, all is true;
Ocean and sky with their blending blue.

'All that wends from its type at will
Is found in some higher harmony still.

'Leaves deformed on the twig I see,
But all meet well in the spreading tree.

'All is beautiful, all is fit,
One creature alone seems wrong in it—

'The creature Man, the being accurst,
Unstable, unmeeting,—the weakest and worst.

'All things together seem fitly grown,
But that monster wanders unplaced and alone.'

Infinite worlds at the music woke
When to the Dæmon the Maker spoke.

'Thine is the mission with pain and strife,
To labour that death may awake to life.

'Ever denying, destroying,—the fight
Turns falsehood and darkness to truth and light.

'But all the battles thy craft e'er span
Will be naught to thy strife with that creature Man.

'For he alone in creation's range
Possesses the endless power of *change.*

'And when the tortures of change are past,
He will conquer all things and thee at last.'

Infinite worlds at the jarring stirred,
When the first-born laughter in life was heard.

And the Dæmon laughed: 'Thou hast given me skill
To strengthen life with power to kill;

'And may I die in my own wild wrath
If I force not Man to a single path!

'My own full power I never have seen
To show what agony, suffering, mean;

'And all my power together I'll draw,
But Man shall walk in a single law.'

In later ages on Mount Meru,
Again time gazed on the fearful Two.

Slowly the centuries ebbed away:
At the foot of the Maker the Dæmon lay.

Adown his head the Denier bent:
'I have worked in all things—my course is spent—

'And Man—thy creature—has conquered me
For ever—*Vicisti Galilæ!*'

DE APIBUS MORTEM DOMINÆ LUGENTIBUS

THE sky is grim, the air is grey,
  There is no gossamer on the grass ;
In shadows dim the vine-leaves swing,
Softly browning and goldening,
  And curling aside that the grapes may pass ;
The grapes which all summer were lurking unseen,
Green themselves in their drapery green.
  Now they are purple and scented sweet,
    And hang like bags of unmade wine :
  Long may they hang, for they never will greet
    Again in the morning that form divine
    Of a beautiful girl now dead and gone,
      Whose hands should have pressed
      From each purple breast
    Wine royal,—the Porphyrogeniton.

      So still and strange !
      So grave and slow !
  It seems as if all things must ever be so
  In a world which only spirits know ;
      Is that a sound
      In the garden's bound
      Or a sigh just dreamed,
      So soft and low ?
  Yes—it is coming—a wondrous humming,
  A weirdly, mournful Elfin drumming,
      Rising and dying,
      Then silent lying ;

The saddest sound upon earth below
A murmur of grief for a maiden gone,
And the bees are mourning Melittion.

There was no human eye to weep
When the lonely girl laid down to sleep
And die,—a humble Dacian slave,
Far cast by war—into a grave.
Yet she was ever good and mild,
And softer spoken than a child;
And when her daily work was done
She loved to wander by the corn
Singing, yet understood by none,
A murmuring lay
Which died away
In a sigh forlorn.
Then rose in a melody sweet and warm,
Buzzing and humming quaintly dull,
Droning and rolling and wonderful
Whispering, hushing, lulling, soft
In solemn tones and dying thrills,
Honeyed and hive-like, fading oft
Like a twilight song from distant hills.
And as she sang, with waving arm,
If they asked her what the song might be,
She said it was called the Wild Bee's Charm,
And her mother sang it beyond the sea,
And the Spirit Ladies who flit through the corn
Had taught her of old the melody.

Twilight and eve
They murmur and grieve,
Humming and drumming mournfully,
Wailing—for they have lost their head,
And the Dacian Queen-Bee Girl is dead.

DE SPIRIDIONE EPISCOPO.

THIS is the story of Spiridion,
Bishop of Cyprus by the grace of God,
Told by Ruffinus in his history.

A fair and stately lady was Iréne,
Spiridion's daughter, and in all the land
Was none so proud, if that indeed be pride,
The haughty conscience of great truthfulness
Which makes the spirit faithful unto death
And martyrdom itself a little thing.

There came a stranger to Spiridion,
A wealthy merchant from the Syrian land,
Who, greeting, said, 'Good father, I have here
A golden casket filled with Roman coin,
And Eastern gems of cost uncountable.
Great are the dangers of the rocky road,
False as a serpent is the purple sea,
And he who carries wealth in foreign lands
Carries his death too often near his heart,
And finds life's poison where he hoped to find
Against its pains a pleasant antidote.
I pray you keep for me these gems in trust
And give them to me when I come again.'

Spiridion listened with a friendly smile,
And answered thus the dark-browed Syrian:
'Here is a better guardian of gold :—

My daughter, Sir. The people round about
Are wont to say that if she broke her faith
Silver and gold themselves would lose their shine.
She is our island's trusty treasurer:—'
'Then,' said the Syrian, 'she shall be mine
As well as theirs'—and saying this he gave
The casket with the jewels to her hand.
Then thoughtfully the lady answered him,
As one who slowly turns some curious thought,
And as they sometimes speak who prophesy:—
'Sir, you have called this treasure life and death,
Which in your Eastern lore, as I have read,
Is the great symbol of the deity,
And the most potent spell to sway the world.
With life to death I'll guard the gems for you,
And dead or living give them back again.'

Now, while the merchant went to distant Rome
The fair Irené died a sudden death,
And all the land went mourning for the maid;
And on the roads and in the palaces
Was one long wail for her by night and day.
While thus they grieved the Syrian came again,
And after fit delay, in proper time
Went to the father:—to Spiridion;
Condoling with him on his daughter's death
In many a sad and gentle Eastern phrase
Deep tinctured with a strange philosophy.

Now, when they had awhile consumed their grief,
Outspoke the Bishop: 'Syrian, it is well
If this sad death be not more sad for us
Than thou hast dreamed of.' Here he checked his speech,
And then, as if in utter agony,
Burst forth with: 'She is gone—and all thy store,
It too is gone—She only, upon earth,

Knew where 'twas hidden, and she trusted none:
Oh, God be merciful! what shall I do?'

Then on him gravely looked the Syrian
With grand calm mien, as almost pitying,
And said, 'Oh, father,—can this be thy *faith?*
Man of the West, how little did'st thou know
The wondrous nature of that girl now dead!
Hast thou not heard that they who once become
Faithful to death are masters over death,
And here and there on earth a woman lives
Whose eyes proclaim the mighty Victory won?
Give me thy hand, and lead me to the dead—
Thou know'st it is not all of death to die.'

He took his hand, and led him to the bier,
And they beheld the Beautiful in Death,
The perfect loveliness of Grecian form,
Inspired by Egypt's solemn mystery:
A single pause in the eternity
Of Present, Past, and Future all in one.

Awhile they stood and gazed upon the dead,
And then Spiridion spoke as one inspired:
'Oh God! thou wert our witness—make it known!'
He paused in solemn awe, for at the word
There came an awful sign. The dead white hand
Was lifted, and Irené's eyes unclosed,
Beaming with light as only angels beam,
And from the cold white lips there came a voice:
'The gems lie hidden in the garden wall;
God bless thee, father, for thy constant love!
God bless thee, Syrian, for thy faith in me!'

This is the story of Spiridion,
And of his daughter, faithful unto death.

POEMS OF PERFUMES.

EAU DE COLOGNE.

THE beautiful Queen of Hungary,
A sad and weary woman was she,
Since for many weeks a terrible pain
Seemed burning and darting through her brain.
Long were the nights, for little she slept;
Longer the days, for all day she wept;
Wretched as woman with pain could be
Was the beautiful Queen of Hungary.

Nothing at all could the doctors do,
Though they searched their folios through and through;
And the wonder was as the weeks went by,
That of such torment she did not die.
But her Majesty had a will of her own,
And a brave little heart as ever was known,
And very determined to live was she,
The beautiful Queen of Hungary.

Finding all pharmacy false and fair,
Her Majesty took to penance and prayer,
'Blessed Otilia, aid me!' she cried:
'Sweet Juliana, be thou my guide!'
For these are the saints whom the Church has said
Should be called upon for a pain in the head,
So she went to them for a remedy:
The beautiful Queen of Hungary.

Long she prayed, till at length it seemed
That though still waking and praying she dreamed.
All around shone a living light
Of angels in angels gleaming bright,
A glory of faces in all the air,
Each blended of faces still more fair,
And rapt in this radiant mystery,
Was the beautiful Queen of Hungary.

But where the splendour brightest shone
Two fairer figures stood gazing down
On the suffering Queen with a loving air,
The two she had called on in her prayer ;
Oh ! the fondest lover has never known
Such beauty in her he would call his own,
And on earth such light you could never see
As shone on the Queen of Hungary.

Saint Juliana the silence broke,
And thus to the kneeling lady spoke:
'Long hast thou suffered—'tis time to know
The pleasure which comes when torments go.
Mary the Mother is Rose of Heaven,—
By the Rosa Mystica life is given ;
Take, in her name, of rose-mary,
Oh, penitent Queen of Hungary !

'Then of Melissa, the honeyed balm,
Which soothed of old the martyr's qualm,
Spirit of rose from the garden bower,
Of fresh sweet mint and the orange-flower,
Blended together these scents give forth
The freshest fragrance known on earth ;
And since it was first revealed to thee,
They shall call it the water of Hungary.'

The heavenly recipé was tried
With great success, and far and wide
Men boasted much of its power to cure,
And said that in headaches 'twas ever sure.
With time some changes o'er it came,
Till at last they changed its very name,
Yet 'tis true enough, and to many known,
That this was the first of Eau de Cologne,
So whenever you use it grateful be
To the sainted Queen Elsa of Hungary.

FRANGIPANI.

WHILE Mutio da Frangipani chose
To walk on earth and lead the course called life,
Men said he was a mighty alchemist,
The greatest master of all mystic lore;
And yet they never feared him. Where he went
All women smiled, and men held out their hands,
Or gave him kindest greeting. One could tell,
In street or hall, where Frangipani stood
By the gay group around him, and the laugh
Reëchoing his own—but his, indeed,
Ah, that was laughter like a Grecian god's,
Deep, resonant, and wild as the full bay
Of Odin's hounds—and when that laugh was heard
The sick would raise their eyelids and exclaim,
'We shall be well, for Frangipani comes!'
And then the nurse would add: 'Yes, when he comes
My labour will be ended. Faith, I think
That Frangipani's shadow is worth more
Than any doctor, body, soul, and all,
Who walks the streets of Rome. Ah, there's a man
Who does not dread the poor. Yet he's a lord,
One of our oldest, noblest families,
And true unto its name. Did you ne'er hear
How centuries ago there lived a count
So full of kindness and all charity

That when a famine came he gave his gold
Unto the poor, until one loaf of bread
Was all remaining to him, and of this
He gave a beggar half, and gained thereby
The name, so famous in our history,
Of Frangipani—"he who breaks the bread"?
This picture hangs in the south-western hall
Of their old palace; and 'tis very strange
How greatly it resembles Mutio,
Who passes all his time in doing good.'
This was his reputation, but his ways
Were little like the ways of those who live
Deep in the darkest learning. Dance and song
Were merrier for his presence. Once he gave
An honest inn-keeper, whose trade was dull,
The recipé for that great cordial
Ros Solis or rosoglio—'the sundew,'
Of musk and coriander and sweet seeds
Well steeped in good red wine of Italy.
A cordial which made the landlord rich,
And then went forth o'er all the Christian world
As a most excellent and Christian drink,
Well suited unto ladies. Truly, he
Was greatly loved by *them*, and 'twas not strange,
Although the stories were which people told
Of his most liberal friendship. Thus 'twas said
That ten brief words once whispered in the ear
Of Clara di Savelli in a dance
Taught her a secret which prolonged her youth
Full forty years. And when she died at last,
She looked into her mirror, with a smile
At her still wondrous beauty, and exclaimed,
'I need not die were Frangipani here:
Yet—do not send for him. I'm tired of play,
And need a little rest. Tell him I'll come
On earth again some day to visit him.

There came a strange disease o'er Italy,
What 'twas we know not—but it vexed men sore,
Till Frangipani found a remedy
Exceeding pleasant, sweet as summer flowers:
A perfumed powder in a velvet bag
Inhaled from hour to hour. It was a cast
Of odours rare—of orris mixed with spice,
Sandal and violet, with musk and rose
Combined in due proportion. Thus he made
The first bouquet of scents. The malady
Soon passed away—the remedy remains,
And with it lives the alchemist's great name
In most enduring fragrance, for he said
'Twas Frangipani's legacy to all
The ladies of all time; he loved them so,
That he would have his name for ever breathed
By them as 'twere a spirit 'mong the flowers.

SWEET MARJORAM.

AMARACOS the beautiful was page,
Or, as some say, the son of Cinyras,
A famous hero in the morning time
Of history, when history was a dream,
And gods meant passions, feelings, scents, and sounds,
And kings and queenly girls and children fair
Acted with singing flowers and talking birds,
Strange fairy tales of nature's mysteries.
Cinyras in the isle of Cyprus served
As the high-priest of Venus. Very dear
To him was her great name, and all her rites
Were as the very spirit of his soul,
For he had looked on beauty through all lands,
And cast his worship starward in the night
Through the dark violet heaven—and in all
Had found that by her power all things drew
Together and *made life*;—yea, death itself
Was but a pause to leap to life again;
And therefore by much study of this thought
It seemed to him the chiefest end of life
To honour her, and this he taught his son;
The pride and glory of the services
Of Aphrodite's temple filled his soul.

Love leads to present rapture,—then to pain,
But all through Love in time is healed again.

There was a grand procession to the shrine
On the great festival, when, as they say,
A voice is heard upon the silent hills
Through all the world, yea, and through all the worlds,
Proclaiming worship to the Queen of Love.
And in the train upon this holy day,
Most beautiful among the beautiful
Went young Amáracos. His office was
To bear the precious Alabaster vase
Which in the olden time had come to earth,
Soft borne by doves unto the Cyprian shrine,
A gift from Venus to her worshippers.
What was within the vase no sage could say,
But this they knew, it gave a sweet perfume
Unlike all fragrant odours known on earth,
And every one did deem himself most blessed
Who could inhale it. Therefore he who bore
The vase was in great honour. All the lords
Of all the land came smiling to the boy,
Each seeking by his courtesy to inhale
The sacred breath of Venus, for they deemed
The mystic vase sent forth an aura sweet
Like that which hangs around the dame divine;
And as he went, bearing his sacred charge,
Hearing his beauty praised by young and old,
Full of the glory of tbe loveliness
In which he lived, to which his life was given,
Pride swelled within his heart, yet scarce had risen,
When, lo! a wild dove from a wood near by,
Dashed boldly on the wing close to his head:
Yes—flapped her pinions in his very face,
And he, all startled by this portent strange,
Let fall the vase—he felt it slip—in vain!
A fright like sickness flashed across his soul:
Down went the vase and shattered on the ground.
One long loud wail rose from the gentle boy,

And instant agony thrilled all the crowd
At this most dark disaster. Then they saw
Amáracos fall down upon the earth
Dead to the heart, but even as he fell
He vanished from their sight, and with him went
The fragments of the vase. Nothing remained,
But on the earth a new-grown herb there stood
Beside a mantle, and its leaves gave forth,
Richer and sweeter than the vase had done,
The self-same sacred fragrance, which is called
The scent Amárakine. The plant grew well,
And others throve from it in every land.
A better gift from Venus than the first :—
And maidens call it the Sweet Marjoram.

JESSAMINE.

AN ARAB POEM.

THE secret mystery of the Jessamine
Sung by an Arab poet long ago,
Azzodmo'l Moccádesi the sage,
Among the voices of the Morning Land.

'*Jas* in the Arab language is despair,
And *Min* the darkest meaning of a lie.
Thus cried the Jessamine among the flowers,
' How justly doth a lie
Draw on its head despair!
Among the fragrant spirits of the bowers
The boldest and the strongest still was I.
Although so fair,
Therefore from Heaven
A stronger perfume unto me was given
Than any blossom of the summer hours.

'And there is nothing unto me so sweet
As to be borne from loving friend to friend
When minutes chase the minutes ever fleet,
And the beginning seems too near the end.
Then I cast all my secret treasure forth,
And she who puts me in her bosom finds,
The warmer place she gives, the better worth,
The odour sweeter than the summer winds,
Bestowed by me upon each pleasant breast
Between the pillows where I had my rest.

'Where'er I go I make my secret known
  And cast my sweet aroma all around,
And the most delicate and gifted own
  That in my breath a fresher life is found.
    But chiefly I delight
When anxious passion wakened to a glow
  By my seductive fragrance flames to fire,
And eyes meet eyes and souls each other know,
  Even to rapture all ineffable
      Which nothing knew before,
    And lips to lips are given
      As souls in heaven
        They—go—
        To bliss
  And in one long sweet passionate gasp expire!

'Among the flowers no perfume is like mine;
  That which is best in me comes from within.
So those who in this life would rise and shine
  Should seek internal excellence to win.
And though 'tis true that falsehood and despair
  Meet in my name, yet bear it still in mind
That where they meet they perish. All is fair
  When they are gone, and nought remains behind.'

ROSE PERFUME.

JIZCHACH BEN AKIBA the Cabalist,
The Emperor Rudolph's friend and favourite,
Dwelling at Prague, determined to resist
The power of death, however he might smite,
Therefore he charmed all metals, beasts, and men,
All hills and rivulets, all rocks and trees,
The reeds which rustled by the oozy fen,
All birds which ran or soared or skimmed the seas,
That none of them should harm him, and at last,
When he had made the mighty list complete,
He proudly cried, 'The hour will soon be past,
And Azrael lie conquered at my feet!'
With this he plucked a rose, but as he smelt
Its fragrance knew that death had reached his heart,
And saw the awful shade who never knelt
To king or magian, standing with his dart:
'How hast thou dared,' he cried, 'to use that flower,
Against my life, when by the mighty charm
Of God 'twas bound to spare me from thy power,
And never yield itself to do me harm?'
'Son,' said the angel, 'it is not the rose
Which kills thee, but the rose's sweet perfume.
The wine is not the goblet whence it flows,
The fragrance not the blossom or its bloom.
'Twas through that fragrance that I reached thy brain;
But hadst thou charmed the perfume with thy spell
I could have used the perfume's life again,
Or that life's spirit, as thou know'st full well.
And still beyond, the subtle tinctures seven,
Which spread in circles infinite to heaven.

SWEET BASIL.

Quo mollius eo suavius.
'The softer the sweeter.'

THE state of Genoa was strong and proud,
So was the Duke of Milan, and the pair
Fell to disputing trifles, and to talk
Of war, as dogs ere fighting show their teeth,
And growl with savage boast before they bite.

But ere it came to blows the Genoese,
At least, the wiser of their senators,
Summoned the man most learned in the law
Of all their land, Francesco Marchio,
And bade him go to Milan and the Duke,
And call on him for speedy settlement
Of all the points disputed. So he went,
And was received with that great courtesy,
And very liberal hospitality,
Which all the great in station, or in soul,
Show unto those who stand too near the line
Of enmity to be considered friend,
And yet not near enough to count as foes.

Day after day passed by, and nought was done,
Though oft Francesco Marchio pressed his claim
To be considered. All their answers were—
'We'll see to it—a thousand pardons, Sir!—

Your Excellence is ever in our mind.
The case must be considered. Genoa
Is doubtless a great state, but every state
Has its own time and method—we have ours :
In the mean time we pray you to accept
Our warm assurances of great respect.'—
And so they played the never-ending air
With all the modulations ; which to hear
And not rush forth enraged, to hang himself
Driven to madness by monotony,
Is the great task of every diplomat,
Which once achieved, leads to the height of fame.

A wary, shrewd, old, well-filed Genoese
Was this same Marchio, so he took his time,
Or let the Duke of Milan take it, till
The want of courtesy in the long delay
Had turned against the host. Meanwhile he spread
A busy rumour that the Genoese
Had sent him there but to procrastinate
And hinder settlement, while they themselves
Were gathering men and arms to go to war.

When this fine tale went buzzing through the town,
There came a speedy summons from the Duke
To Marchio, and the cunning councillor
Hastened to heed the bidding. But few words
Had passed between them ere Francesco held
Some twigs of fair sweet-Basil forth, and said,
'I pray your Highness mark this curious herb ;
Touch it but lightly, stroke it softly, Sir,
And it gives forth an odour sweet and rare ;
But crush it harshly and you'll make a scent
Most disagreeable. So with Genoa,—
Handle it gently, 'tis all gentleness,
But treat it rudely, 'twill be rude in turn.'

The speech, 'tis said, impressed the Ducal host,
And soon the ambassador, full-satisfied,
Returned to Genoa. The state, well-pleased,
Gave him sweet-Basil for his coat-of-arms
As a reward, and for a motto put
Quo mollius eo suavius in his shield.

MANY IN ONE.

A POEM IN THREE PARTS.

MYTHICAL, MEDIÆVAL, MODERN.

PART I.

MYTHICAL.

BEL ER OPH ADON,
First of enchanters
In the old moon time,
Lord of the Fire Land,
Plougher of Orcus,
Scarlet-born, Sun-born,
Azure-born, Sea-born,
Purple-born, King-born,
Learned in all magic—
By long endurance,
Penance, and torture
From the abysses
Of Godhood tremendous,
Gained him such power,
Wrenched forth such glory:
Never was mortal
Clad in such beauty,
Forced from the Æons,
From the abysses,

Terrible beauty,
Loveliness fearful,
Splendour of ages ;—
Such was his form.

Bel Er Oph Adon
Rose in the evening,
Purple and rose-glown
Light was around him,
Fairer the radiance
Shed from his features ;
Back on the sunset,
Back on the purple,
Splendour o'er splendour,
Beauty o'er beauty
Flashes his god-light.
Bel Er Oph Adon
Goes to his bridal ;
She, the great Star Queen,
Venus the golden,
Ivory, crimson,
Waits for his coming,
Waits for his beauty,
She, the Immortal,
Seeks his embraces,
In her pavilion
Flashes celestial
Ray forth her raptures.
All through the night time
Quivers the North Light ;—
So love the Gods.

Thus spoke the Star Queen :
'Bel Er Oph Adon,
Thou who of mortals
Only hast mastered

Æons unnumbered,
Tinctures of beauty
Over the earth-born,
E'en to the glories
Which my earth kingdom
Shows not to mortals.
Lord of enchanters,
Say, can thy magic,
Can thy ambition
Picture more honour
Than the sweet rapture
God-given, God-flowing,
Of my embraces?
Know'st thou in Orcus?
Know'st thou aught earthly?
Know'st thou in ocean?
Know'st thou in air life?
Or in the ages
Coming or vanished,
Aught like this pleasure?
Answer my soul.'

Thus to the Star Queen
Answered the Magus:
'Fairer than thou art
Never was Goddess,
Sweeter or dearer,
And in the ages
Flowing and coming,
All shades of heaven
Onward for ever
Know of no rapture
Like thy embraces.
Yet if thou seekest
Thus I must answer;—
Truth is my power,

By truth I ascended ;—
And I am prouder
That each great goddess
In the great kingdoms
Made me her lover.
Deep in the darkness
Far among shadows,
By the pale Empress
Splendid in horror,
Fearful in beauty,
Long time I lingered.
Oft in the Spring-tide
On the green mountain
Came to me, kissed me,
Under dark branches,
Hid from the moonlight,
Dioné the fair.

Baaltis the Ancient,
Queen of the Mountains,
Glowing gold-lustred,
Breathing hot perfumes,
Sparkling in splendour,
Pantherine graceful,
Lost in black tresses
Like a white swan
On the Stygian river,
Wooed me in madness,
Wooed me and won me ;
So did Astarté,
Lady of Fire Land,
So did Melitta
Mel Ida, Meldea,
She of the Sun-realm
Queen of the orgy,
Fearful and passionate,

Secret and sacred.
Eastward or Westward,
Heaven-born—earthly,
All the great beauties
Worshipped by mortals,
All have caressed me.
Thee I have best loved ;
Yet since thou askest
What makes me proudest,
Truly I answer
All make me proud.'

Thus answered Venus,
Fair Aphrodité,
Rose-tinted sea foam:
'That which we love best
Should make us proudest.
Never should true love
From pride be dissevered,
And in thy love now
Shall both be united.
Listen to secrets
Awful and charming ;
When in the shadows
Deep in the caverns
Lovely Persephoné
Clasped thee with kisses,
I was thy loved one.
When on the mountain
Stately Dioné
In thy embraces
Made the leaves rustle,
I was thy beauty,
Bow-bearing, moon-horned.
I was Baältis,
Morning land-splendoured,

Serpentine twining,
Glowing in glory,
Passionate lovely,
Many and One.

'I was all others,
All who have loved thee ;
White Anaïtis
Loveliness flowing,
Limbs like milk rivers ;
Also Melitta.
Goddess of Sweetness,
Honey and perfume,
Terrible pleasures
Are her embraces.
Infinite thrilling
The luscious arcana
Taught in her orgies,
Flashed in her glances :—
Yet was Melitta
The ray of my spirit,
And with the goddess
And in the goddess
Thou wert with me love.
High in the heavens,
On the green mountains,
Deep in hell's palace,
I the One Only
Held thee in rapture,
Ever enjoying
Thy faith in the Many,
Even as thou in
Thy faith wert delighted ;
Now thou hast all, love ;
Now thou hast learned love,
All is in love.'

PART II.

MEDIÆVAL.

BE'T far or near,
Dark tales we hear
    How Satan wins the soul
Of those who fain
Would wisdom gain,
    Or yield to Love's control;
Yet well I wete
That wisdom great
    Ne'er caused a soul to fall,
And those who sin
True love to win
    Have never sinned at all.

For wisdom high
Can pierce the sky
    To Heaven's brightest bower,
And true love's spell
Send joy through hell,
    Where devils sit in dour;
And ye in doubt
Who stay without,
    Awhile your minds engage,
While I unfold
The story old
    Of Satan and the Sage.

In Italie
Beyond the sea
There lived a man so learned,
All heathen lore
From days of yore
By magic he discerned.
In many a tomb,
In ancient gloom
Unbroke since Jovis sped,
He all day long
With magic song
Held speech with Romans dead.

Each goblin child,
And fairies wild
That in the rivers swim,
And sylphids rare
Who float in air,
Made strange discourse to him.
From antique graves
And hidden caves
Deep murmurings were cast,
And statues white
In dim moonlight
Cried *Salve!* as he passed.

And for such sin
His soul within
Had Satan power to lay
A dismal curse
To turn to worse
As time should pass away.
And that vile root
Which Satan put
To win him from above,

Was this, that he,
From woman free,
    Should ne'er know woman's love.

But oh, what part
Hath devils' art
    In those whom Heaven owns?
Though Satan sing
Till Chaos ring,
    God chants for deeper tones.
The wittiest wile
And subtlest guile
    Ne'er reach the inmost core;
The mouse may know
Shrewd tricks, I trow,
    But ever the cat knows more.

And now this sage
In ripening age
    Felt Cupid's wondrous power,
And oft would dream,
By hill or stream,
    Of love in bed or bower.
Yet all alone
He made his moan,—
    Alone he led his life;
No maiden fair
With him would pair,
    No woman be his wife.

With every spell
And charm from hell
    He tempted girls to guile,
But every May
Still said him Nay,—
    No maid on him could smile.

With gems and gold
Right many a fold
He sought to buy their charms,
But ever the curse
Turned bad to worse:
They died within his arms.

Ah God, what is
All wealth I wis
To him who liveth so?
Withouten love
E'en heaven above
I ween were bitter woe
The fairest flower,
In sun or shower,
Is but a laidly weed,
And so this man
To Satan than
Did turn him in his need.

And the Great Lord
Of ill accord
With him did thus agree:
'A leman fai
Of beauty rare
I straight will give to thee.
But this be known:
To her alone
Shall all thy love be given;
If ever thou change,
And from her range,
Thou ne'er shalt rise to heaven.'

Mark well, O Heart,
What wondrous art
Hath God to guard our youth.

This sage but sought,
By magic taught,
To learn all wisdom's truth.
Great risks they run
Who've thus begun
And walk where shadows reign,
But ever God,
With guiding rod,
Will lead them back again.

Now this fair maid
To him purveyed
Was but a demon fell,
Whom Satan meant
With foul intent
To lure him into hell.
But soon she felt
Her spirit melt,—
Her life with love was sore,
And in her heart
There burned a smart
She never knew before.

From early time
The blackest crime
Had ever been her play ;
In blood and filth
She found her health
And passed the time away.
Even Rome's proud Queen,
Great Messaline,
To her was but a child,
Yet all her soul
In sweet control
Was soon by Love beguiled.

The task she had
As Satan bade
Was this—to make her love
In constant range
To beauties strange,
And still to others rove.
Small wish had she
That this should be,
Or he from her should sever
The man whose faith
Thro' life and death
She fain would keep for ever.

With torture turned
In pain she burned,—
No hope was ever there ;
For all within
Was death and sin,
And hell was everywhere.
Till love so deep
Made angels weep,
It proved a chastening rod ;
Love's suffering
To heaven takes wing :
She dared to think of God.

Then to her mind
By pain refined
A subtle thought came in,
A fancy deep
Her love to keep
And cheat the power of sin.
How this should be
In time you'll see ;
Twas all as Heaven bid.

When prayer we bring
Full many a thing
    Is oft from Satan hid.

One day her love
Had chanced to rove,
    And by the river strayed,
When all away
Mid forests grey
    He met a lovelier maid.
Straight trapt and caught,
He gave no thought
    Unto his leman fond,
And lesser still
His wanton will
    Upon the devil's bond.

In evening breeze,
Beneath the trees,
    They wandered long alone.
In greenwood shade
A tender maid
    Right easily is won.
As the rushes shook
In the bubbling brook
    His heart with passion thrilled,
Each long gold hair
Is subtle snare
    When souls with love are filled.

With many a kiss
Of burning bliss
    They part, and true love swear;
But when next day
He came that way
    He found another there.

A cream-white queen
Of stately mien
    With eyes like midnight stars.
For her in turn
His passions burn
    And naught his longing bars.

And thus for years,
Withouten fears,
    He led a wanton life,
And aye his will
Did he fulfil
    With many a lovely wife.
Full many a maid
In greenwood shade,
    Full many a bird in bower,
And ladies great
Of high estate
    Had he for paramours.

Time fleeth on,
Youth soon is gone,
    Naught earthly may abide ;
Life seemeth fast,
But may not last,—
    It runs as runs the tide.
A shallop bark
Ye oft may mark
    Well anchored firm and sound ;
But lest it flies
When waters rise
    'Tis by the anchor drowned.

Thus to our sage
In later age
    There came the broken bowl ;

His wasted youth
And broken truth,
    And then his forfeit soul.
No joy of wine
Or concubine
    Could heal his growing sore;
Cold shadows vast
Around him passed,
    And all was hell before.

Thus oft alone
He made his moan
    Mid rocks and forests grim,
Till once when there,
He was aware
    Of one who came to him,—
A lady bright,
While rosy light
    Shone round as she did pass,
Like diamonds on
The thistle down,
    And glow-worms in the grass.

'Sweet heart,' she cried,
'Dost know thy bride?
    Thy love of early years?
The first whom thou
Did'st kiss, comes now
    To drive away thy fears.'
'Ah, God,' said he,
'How can that be,
    When I am all forlorn?
My soul is lost,
My fate is crost,
    There's none so wretched born.'

As when black clouds,
Like fearful shrouds,
Are blown by reckless wind,
And glad we mark
The fleeting dark
With golden light behind;
Or nightmare grim,
Which froze each limb,
Is driven by loving kiss,
E'en so the word
Which next he heard
Did bring him back to bliss.

'Thou dream'st,' she spoke,
'The bond is broke,
And all thy soul is gone,
Because that thou
Did'st quit thy vow
And leave me all alone.
'Twas Satan's will;
But Heaven still
Hath deeper love than he.
In others' arms,
By other charms,
Thou ever wert with me.

'As thou did'st range,
So I did change
To bodies young and fair,
Of tawny hue,
Or fresh and new,
To white with golden hair.
Was't Pernel, Joane,
Or Josiane,
Or Blanche, or Marinel,

Or Florens sweet,
Or Marguerite,
    I was thy bonnibel.

'Yes; I, the Elf,
Was still myself,
    Though wooed in many a form;
And ever anon
I still came on,
    And got thy kisses warm.
Though thou did'st fly
Like bird in sky,
    Yet faster still I flew,
And only one
Was thine alone,
    And thou wert ever true.

'The work is done,
Thy soul is won;
    I too am saved from thrall,
Since now my yoke
In hell is broke,
    For true love conquers all.
We may not rise
To yonder skies
    For many an age, I see;
But thou art mine,
And I am thine,
    And saved through love of thee.'

Two eagles flew
Through heaven blue,—
    May well such wonder be.
Two wild deer strayed
Through greenwood shade,
    Two fish swam in the sea.

From life to life,
Sweet dear and wife,
    I ween we often rove,
But never part
When once the heart
    Has found its own true love.

PART III.

MODERN.

I WANDER in a wildering dream.
    What meaneth this, what meaneth all?
    Lord Arion with his dolphin call?
And steam-boats on old sacred streams?

What is this mystery which I hate?
    Are dirt and steam the life to live?
    Must I the inner truth up-give
With gold-fire interpenetrate?

I stand beside a mud canal,
    I hear six costermongers cry:
    The iron road like snakes goes by,
Yet the old sun shines over all.

There is primæval loveliness,
    And here is nothing of the kind;
    New wisdom drives the soul to wind,
And all is one infernal mess.

When Dante sat upon his stone
    In Florence, then the world was square.
    He knew just how to strike them there,
But now who knows the age's tone?

'Twas better when in Sodom thou
    Saw'st God on this side, hell on that
    In an arena fair and flat;
But say—where is the devil now?

I know a man whose heart is whole,
    In the great city of New York ;
    He deals in stocks and meal and pork :
May God have mercy on my soul !

Were he but Ser Porcone hight !—
    And did he but a ducat owe
    To sainted Fra Angelico
For painting San Antonio bright !

How very easy 'twould have been
    To tell the legend of my friend,
    Illuminated to the end,
As though 'twere drawn from Voragin !

Yet will I tell it as I may,
    Although I be a traitor hight,
    Gone back on the Pre-Raphael light—*
Like the Great Lord of Paint—Millais.

This man I knew, whose name was Smith,
    By Fate's sharp scalpel lost his wife,
    The oyster of his hard shell life,
And of his plant the very pith.

He mourned her taken up to Heaven
    While wandering in his devious ways ;
    All life a wild and wilful maze,—
And then joined Circle Number Seven.

Thou know'st not what that means ? Then list,—
    Such circles are the only rings
    In which Romance at present springs,
For Smith had turned Spiritualist.

When next I met him, in his eye
    There was a sweet and winky light,
    His very hat and gloves seemed bright
With adolescent ecstasy.

* 'Gone back on' is an *American* term for being renegade.

I gently touched upon his woe,
I took him softly by the hand,
But with a motion like command
He turned upon me and cried, '*Poh!*

'Condole not with me on the dead;
They never die,—they're always here;
They sip with us the foaming beer,
They're at our table,—and in bed.'

''Tis true,' I said. 'Invisible,
The dead are round us everywhere,
But thinner than the thinnest air:'—
Here Smith replied, derisible:

'Such ignorance but makes me laugh,
When yester evening I embraced,
With arms tight locked around her waist,
My dear departed better half.'

'Great Heaven,' I cried, 'how can that be?
Does then the grave return its dead,
And spirits from the portal sped,
Hie backwards from Eternity?'

But Smith replied in calmest tones:
'This spirit of my darling wife,
Who comes so oft to cheer my life,
Had entered into Mary Jones.

'You know her—isn't she divine?
God never made a prettier girl,
A real peach—a perfect pearl—
With cheeks which flash with Heaven's wine.

'I only hope my wife will stay
A long long time in Mary's form;
She says she finds it nice and warm;
Nor change about—as is her way.

'For since she died, beyond a doubt
She's been in mediums—let me see !
Yes, altogether, twenty-three !
'Tis hard to follow her about.

'Yet 'tis not all devoid of fun,
If for an instant you reflect,
That I must treat them with respect,
For all the Twenty-Three are One !

'One spirit, though of different flesh;
But what's the body ? Doctors say
It changes atoms every day,—
Only the soul abideth fresh.

And would you make of Earth a Heaven,
Learn that the body is but dust;
Think not of earthly laws or lust,
And join our Circle—Number Seven.'

A THOUSAND YEARS AGO.

THOU and I in spirit-land,
A thousand years ago,
Watched the waves beat on the strand,
Ceaseless ebb and flow;
Vowed to love and ever love—
A thousand years ago.

Thou and I in greenwood shade,
Nine hundred years ago,
Heard the wild dove in the glade
Murmuring soft and low;
Vowed to love for evermore,—
Nine hundred years ago.

Thou and I in yonder star,
Eight hundred years ago,
Saw strange forms of light afar
In wild beauty glow;
All things change, but love endures
Now as long ago!

Thou and I in Norman halls,
Seven hundred years ago,
Heard the warder on the walls
Loud his trumpet blow,—
'Ton amors sera tojors,'
Seven hundred years ago!

Thou and I in Germany,
  Six hundred years ago—
Then I bound the red cross on:
  'True love, I must go,—
But we part to meet again
  In the endless flow!'

Thou and I in Syrian plains,
  Five hundred years ago,
Felt the wild fire in our veins
  To a fever glow!
All things die, but love lives on
  Now as long ago!

Thou and I in shadow-land,
  Four hundred years ago,
Saw strange flowers bloom on the strand,
  Heard strange breezes blow:
In the ideal love is real,
  This alone I know.

Thou and I in Italy,
  Three hundred years ago,
Lived in faith and died for God,
  Felt the faggots glow:
Ever new and ever true,
  Three hundred years ago.

Thou and I on southern seas,
  Two hundred years ago,
Felt the perfumed even-breeze,
Spoke in Spanish by the trees,
  Had no care or woe:
Life went dreamily in song
  Two hundred years ago.

Thou and I mid Northern snows,
 One hundred years ago,
Led an iron, silent life,
 And were glad to flow
Onwards into changing death,
 One hundred years ago.

Thou and I but yesterday
 Met in Fashion's show,
Love, did you remember me,
 Love of long ago?
Yes; we keep the fond oath sworn
 A thousand years ago!

LEGENDS OF THE BIRDS.

THE WONDERFUL CROW.

Erfordiensis quidam civis corvum in deliciis habuisse dicitur quem spiritum ejusmodi fuisse (i.e. *spiritus aeri*) quod sequitur evincit. Quum quidam die tacitum et tristem videret, 'quid tu,' inquit jocabundus, 'mi corve ita mæstus es; quidve cogitas? Heic ex improviso ingeminat: *Cogitavi dies antiquos et annos æternos in mente habui.* Statimque ex oculis heri disparuit.

'There was a certain citizen of Erfurth who had a pet crow which was one of these spirits of the air, as the following fully proves. For seeing him one day sad and silent, the master said in joke: "Well, my crow, why are you so sorrowful, and of what are you thinking?" To whom the crow mournfully made answer from the seventy-seventh Psalm: "*I have considered the days of old, the years of ancient times.*" Having said this he suddenly disappeared from the eyes of his lord.'—*Henrici Kornmanni. Opera Curiosa Francofurti, A.M.*, A.D. 1694.

IN the Thuringian Land of Song,
Where nightingales sing all summer long,
By the river Gesar Erfurth stands,
A town well-known in many lands;
For there—as all the histories tell—
Great Luther had a cloister cell.
Enough—of him no further word,
My song is of a humbler bird
Than the great Reformation swan,
Whose notes were heard in freedom's dawn.

In this town of Erfurth—long ago
A gentleman once tamed a crow,
Which proved to be a wondrous bird,
If we may trust a writer's word:
For he cawed to the horses in the stable,
Could dance a hornpipe on the table,
Beat time with his bill to the harper's tunes,
Pilfered honey and hid the spoons,
Kissed the maidens and bullied the cats,
Played with the children and chased the rats,
Frolicked about in the kitchen dens
Where he earned a living by driving hens,
Broke with his bill the window panes,
And was always tangled in ladies' trains,
Till everybody declared that he
Was the life and soul of the family.

In the town of Erfurth long ago
A change came over that jolly crow.
No more he heeded the harper's tunes,
No longer he pilfered honey or spoons,
No more to the hens was a constable grim,
And the cats quite lost their awe of him;
While after dinner he danced no more
His 'wheel-about' jigs on table or floor,
And his health and spirits sunk so low
That he seemed to be quite a converted crow.

One day his master jesting said:
'Crow! what fancies are in your head,
Or what mighty sorrow is on your soul,
That you mope and hide like a frightened mole?
Crow, my Crony——'
Here came a surprise!
The master started and opened his eyes,
While a sense of doubt and terror stole o'er him,
As though a ghost had jumped up before him.

Well might he start—for, without a joke,
The crow uplifted his voice and spoke,
In good clear tones, with no awe or qualms,
From the Seventy-seventh of David's Psalms:
'*Cogitavi dies antiquos*'—
(Here he paused)—'*et annos æternos.*'
He spoke with great solemnity,
Setting forth this ancient Chronology;
But ere a second breath they drew
He spread his wings, and away he flew
Far over river and road and plain,
And never in Erfurth was seen again.

MORAL.

'Tis common in every place
To set forth by a crow the negro race,
As Gilmore Simms long years ago
Made known in his tale of The Lazy Crow.
And 'tis very fine, if you are able,
To have them work on your farm or stable,
Dance your jigs and beat your call,
And 'never pay them nothing at all.'
But it cannot last for ever, you know,
For a time will come when every crow,
After being silent and perplexed,
Will search the Scriptures and find a text,—
A text of the wonderful days of old,
When truth was to white and black unrolled,
Then find his tongue. Fire melts all frost;
E'en the negro will find his Pentecost—
And, speaking out, like a soul set free,
Will rise to knowledge and liberty.

Philadelphia, 1863.

THE SWALLOW.

WHEN Jesus hung upon the cross
The birds, 'tis said, bewailed the loss
Of Him who first to mortals taught,
Guiding with love the life of all,
And heeding e'en the sparrows' fall.

But, as old Swedish legends say,
Of all the birds upon that day,
The swallow felt the deepest grief,
And longed to give her Lord relief,
And chirped when any near would come,
'*Hugswala swala swal honom!*'
Meaning, as they who tell it deem,
Oh, cool, oh, cool and comfort Him!

Oh soul, oh life, oh love! Whene'er
A sufferer in this world draws near,
Wilt thou remember ere thou go
How Jesus died in bitterest woe?
That thou in every brother's pain
Might'st see thy Saviour live again.
Then, drawing from the living stream,
'Oh, cool, oh, cool and comfort Him!'

THE SWAN.

WHO rides the rustling woods by night?
  Sweet through the green leaves shines the moon;
Blue flames his steel, his plume is white,
  And the brook is singing an Elfin tune.

His road is running with the stream,
  Sweet through the green leaves shines the moon;
Who wakes in love still walks in dream,
  And the brook is singing an Elfin tune.

Are those three swans white splashing there?
  Sweet through the green leaves shines the moon;
No swans are they, but women fair,
  And the brook is singing an Elfin tune.

On a tree their swan-robes wave and fall,
  Sweet through the green leaves shines the moon;
And the knight, if he would, may seize them all,
  While the brook is singing an Elfin tune.

Who wears a swan-robe merrily,
  Sweet through the green leaves shines the moon;
May sail at will o'er land and sea,
  And the brook is singing an Elfin tune.

He rides and leaves them hanging there:
  Sweet through the green leaves shines the moon;
'When you swim of your clothes take better care,
There are some who would rob you, ladies fair!'
  And the brook is singing an Elfin tune.

He rides into the deadly fight ;
Sweet through the green leaves shines the moon ;
Far o'er him fly three swans so white,
And the brook is singing an Elfin tune.

A lance has killed him in the fray :
Sweet through the green leaves shines the moon ;
Three swans with a soul have flown away ;
They fade in the first red light of day :—
And the brook is singing an Elfin tune.

THE PEACOCK.

WHY has the peacock hideous feet?
Why is his voice no longer sweet?
He who in Eden ere the Fall
Mid birds, in both, surpassed them all.

To Paradise, the Arabs say,
Satan could never find the way
Until the peacock led him in:—
Pride takes in every sin;—
Pride teaches Evil paths to gain
Which he for years had sought in vain.

The curse which pierced the Serpent through,
'Tis said, fell on the peacock too.
His voice, which once in Eden's vales
Rang sweeter than the nightingale's,
Grew harsh:—the feet, which led the way
Of him who led the world astray,
Became the claws which now he wears,
Such as the Hebrew demon bears.

Such is the story, plain to all,
Which teaches, Pride must have a fall.

THE EAGLE.

WHO is ruler of the eagles,
Father of the feathered kings?
In the dark and lonely Norland
There the giant spreads his wings:
Giant bird and god Hrosvelgar;—
As the Iceland poet sings.

When he flaps his wings, a tempest
Howling o'er the ocean flies,
From his eyes the lightning flashes,
And he makes the whirlwind rise:
So he calls his eagle-children,
And they answer him with cries.

'He who clears away corruption,'
Is the meaning of his name;
Storm-winds sweep away infection,
Wrath and strength cure many a shame.
Eagles also have their mission:
Every bird should not be tame!

THE OWL.

WHEN Jesus walked in Jewry, then
He hungered oft like other men ;
And quaint old monkish legends say
That in a baker's shop one day
He asked for food. About to bake,
The mistress took a generous cake,
And said : 'All this I mean for thee ;
Wait, Lord, until it ready be!'
'It is too much!' her daughter cried,
And put one half the gift aside
With angry air. He nothing said,
But by the fire laid down the bread,
When, lo! as when a blossom blows,
To a vast loaf the manchet rose!
In angry wonder standing by,
The girl sent forth a wild, rude cry,
And feathering fast into a fowl,
Flew to the woods a wailing owl!

Each voice which in the desert cries
Teaches a lesson to the wise.
Experience, the mistress stern,
In legends gives us truth to learn,
And emblemed in the owl we see
That all men wise and kind should be.

Thus monks in moralizing strain
Revived Minerva's bird again,
Adding a kindlier Christian sense
To the symbol of intelligence,
Making it Learning's quaintest type
Humanity and wisdom ripe.

TO YOU.

I.

WHEN day's red light is lost in night
  As waking thoughts are lost in dreams,
And fancies flit in wanton flight
  As fire-flies glisten o'er the streams,
And all the perfumes of the flowers
  Have turned to nectar all the air,
What would you do in those sweet hours—
  What *would* you do—if *I* were there?

In greenwood shade 'neath starry shine,
  When singing to the midnight breeze,
You breathe the scent-life of the pine
  And seek wild coverts 'mid the trees;
Wild heart, whose life is all in night!
  Strange dreamer in the leafy lair,
What would you—far from others' sight!
  What *would* you do—if *I* were there?

Full was the moon and high the sea
  In hours when you and I were born;
Blood red the sky gleamed wondrously
  Upon us in the early morn—
It bodes *great hearts and bloody death;*
  But what for that would either care
If when we drew the parting breath
  'Twere hand in hand together there?

I see the full moon overhead,
  I hear the rustle of the pines ;
I see thee live who once wast dead,
  I hear thee singing by the vines :
'Tis *I* myself—for we are one,
  One thought alone and everywhere,
One Night, one Day—one Self, one Sun,
  For we are All—for ever there.

II.

Although I know all earthly forms
  Must meet with earth's decay,
I cannot think thy beauty's life
  Will ever pass away.
When meaner shapes of loveliness
  Return with every rain,
Can I believe that thou wilt fade,
  And never come again ?

When summer warms the forest fair
  Its flowers again will blow,
When winter chills again the air
  Again we'll see the snow :
The brook will flash through emerald grass,
  The star from heaven high—
If lesser beauty cannot pass,
  Can thine, sweet darling, die?

To think the love I feel for thee
  Is love for earth alone,
That were a pain no joy on earth
  Could e'er on earth atone.
The Lord who gave thee to my heart
  Wields no such torturing rod.
Sweet heart, because I live in thee,
  I do believe in God.

Thou dearest of all living things,
  Thou sunshine in my soul,
In thee a light of life upsprings
  Beyond all life's control.
Full many a dungeon gets its light
  From Heaven through narrow bars ;—
To *me* there came an angel bright ;
  —— I thought no more of stars.

III.

Whene'er thou movest, in every part
  There waves a flowing rhyme ;
The life of all the loveliest art
  Which lived in olden time.
And if that art had ever been
  What long it sought to be,
Then men long since in Art had seen
  What still I find in thee.

Whene'er I gaze into thine eyes
  And deep love holds me dumb,
I feel the Past within me rise
  Towards fairer dreams to come.
Then to the Present I am wed,
  The Present bears me on ;
Stars shine the brightest, it is said,
  'Twixt darkness and the dawn.

Whene'er thy fingers sweep the chords,
  Whatever thou hast played,
My heart sweet-suffering seeks the words,
  Those words which ne'er were made.
And though full many a golden phrase
  In many a tongue may sound,
And poets rise to angel lays,
  Those words will ne'er be found.

The Past is in thy grace, sweetheart,
The Present in thine eyes,
But in thy voice the Future thrills
With all its harmonies.
Thou showest God in calm or mirth,
There is a promise given
In thy deep eyes, that love on earth
Means endless joy in Heaven.

TO RISE WITH THEE!'

THEY said it to me until I believed,
And then I said it sadly to myself;
'The yearning for the Beautiful is vain;
Art is a bauble, Pride a stumbling-block,
And your brave, Noble Soul, a silly dupe,
While all must yield to selfish Common Sense,
To Common Sense and Gold. In this believe!
And in my need and grievous loneliness,
Amid the dust and turmoil of the land,
I *did* believe;—when, lo! I heard a voice
As of youth singing on the distant hills,
And then there came the gleam of glorious eyes,
The tramp of steeds, the rush of autumn winds,
And memories of those ideal friends
Dreamed in the days of hope, and last of all
The pale, proud, glorious face of their great Queen,
Like Lucifer's when reconciled to God,—
Too grand for woman, yet too sweet for man,
Nobler from knowledge—better from the fall,
And then I wept and turned to Truth again.

The past is but a mouldering shroud,
The future all a shimmering cloud;
But thy proud glance, oh! queenly star
Turns not to phantoms faint and far.

Thou lov'st to hear the North Wind's song,
To see the torrent foam along.
Oh! could I dart as wild and free
For ever on, proud heart, with thee!

The mists of dawn drive fast and far,
And dimmer grows the morning-star;
I see the day's red life arise,
Reflected back from thy deep eyes;
All moves and lives 'mid wakening sounds,
And glad with life thy brave heart bounds;
Thou gallant, daring heart, how free
That heart must bound which mates with thee!

Souls love! What though it be not given
To us to dart like sprites through heaven,
Or float in torrent-whirls along
Forgetting life in one wild song,
Still we may scorn the slavish fears
Which crush the world to doubts and tears,
And they who win this strength rise free
With falcon glance o'er heaven and sea.

And thou hast won it. Strength by strength
Thou'st conquered all the spell at length.
Henceforth no coward fear can chill,
No lies benumb the joyous will,
And all things unconfined and free
Sing one great song of life to thee.

And who is she who woke the song?
Oh friend, look forth! In every throng
Thou seest some eye which proudly gleams
As though awaked from earth's low dreams,

Some yearning glance in which is seen
What fain would be—what might have been.
A glance which, when I feel and see,
My heart burns wild 'to rise with thee.'

ALMA VENUS.

THERE were two Christians drowning in a storm,
And unto them came Venus in her light,
Who offered to the first a helping hand:
But he preferred to drown, too pious far
To owe his life to her. Then to the next
She turned in beauty, and he took her hand.
When safe upon the shore he kneeling cried:
'I thank thee as the minister of God,
Fair Queen of Loveliness and Life and Love.
Since He hath chosen thee to save my life
Shall I pass judgment on His ways and means?'
The first who drowned went unto Heaven's gate,
And knocked, and there could hardly enter in,
So close St Peter held the leaf—the next
Found it wide open with a welcome cry.
God is in all things, and he works through all.

THE ORIGIN OF WHEAT.

BLESSED are they whose hearts and heads are full
Of golden legends of the olden time,
What is well tried need not be tried again.

For they shall walk through life as in a dream,
And rocks and grass and grain shall all be charmed.
Were bird-songs needless, birds would never sing.

Know'st thou the story how the bearded wheat,
Man's friendliest food, came unto earth with him ?
Who knows what destiny runs by his own ?

When Adam fell with Eve from Eden's bowers
No spirit of the flowers would go to earth.
Those who have fallen keep no rising friends.

Only the wheat, which hitherto was held
Of little worth, went to the world with them.
Who knows what bough may save a drowning man ?

Bread is the staff of life, and wheat the type ;
As man is buried, so the wheat is sown.
The ancient sacrament is bread and wine.

Think of all this when next you sow or reap,
Or gather into barns the golden grain.
No work was ever hindered yet by song.

6

SONG OF THE NEW YEAR.

OUT from the North, where ice and snow
Hold one eternal carnival,
Whirling with tempests as they blow,
While deadly frost is over all,
Just newly born,
Unstained, unworn
With light for life-blood fast I fly;
Lord of the hours
With sun or showers,
King of the Year—lo! here am I!

And I am of your lives a part,
Your very selves—remember well!
I beat in every bounding heart,
And grow in every flower and shell.
The roaring sea
Is blue with me;
Each oak-ring with its circled rhyme
Repeating what
The last year taught,
All chronicle my round of time.

The mighty mountains know my hand,
The tides all count me hurrying on;
New born, new dead, in every land;
Record me coming—show me gone;

The rocks and graves,
The flowers and waves,
The lonely plains, where all is drear,
With ruins old
And loves untold,
All tell the story of the year.

The silent forms that flit around
Man's daily doings, out and in:
Unborn to sight, unkin to sound,
Free from the shade of sense or sin;
To them each hour
An awful power
More than to mortal man I seem.
They count my bounds,
And know the rounds
Scarce glimmering in a Plato's dream.

The lovely face with golden hair
Which seemed to thee a world divine;
The graceful arms—the all too fair,
I swear by truth shall all be thine!
What doth appear
On earth most dear
Is all a promise made below,
When it hath slept
It will be kept
In the fair rose-life yet to blow.

All this I mark—all this I am,
I die, but I shall live again;
I rise in every choral psalm,
I vanish with the ripened grain,
Then though we die
Sing loud--fill high!

And be your laughter brave and long!
The year's great power
Is in each hour;
All time is but a New Year song!

IN THE NORTH.

THE moonlight shines upon the waves
  All bending in the wind ;
The sail-boat runs before them both,
  But leaves her foam behind.

The porpoise takes the tide to sea,
  The herring to the sand ;
The seagull fishes far away,
  But rests at night on land.

And if you say 'tis time to go,
  I'm off to sea once more ;
But if your eyes should tell me 'No,'
  I'll stay to-night on shore.

The tide runs up, the tide runs down,
  The waves they rise and fall ;
But with a man whose mind is set
  It's once and once for all.

IN THE SOUTH.

HEY up the river,
  And ho ! down the bay !
Trees on the black rock,
  And grass on the grey.
Send the boat closer in,
  Up to the shore ;
There she is standing,
  Just holding the door !
Now is the time
  If you've something to say ;
Hey up the river,
  And ho ! down the bay !

Something is coming,
  I know by her smile ;
'Let me go down with you,
  Only a mile ?'
'Plenty of room
  For a dozen like you :—
More to the forward,
  And trim the canoe !
Now we are off again,
  Well under weigh ;
Hey up the river,
  And ho ! down the bay !'

Out of the deep water
  Into the shoal,
Lay down the paddle,
  And take up the pole!
Pull by the bushes!
  Look out for the root!
Into the current,
  And over the shoot!
'Keep on another mile?'
  'Just as you say!'
Hey up the river,
  And ho! down the bay!

'When the moon rises,
  We'll go by her light.'
Still she kept on with him
  All through the night:
Two miles, and three miles,
  And five miles, and ten:
Back to the river home
  Never again.
Long was the journey,
  But short seemed the way;
Hey up the river,
  And ho! down the bay!

Elk River, Braxton County, West Virginia,
May 20, 1866.

THE DREAM

'Life's sweetest dreams
Are foam on streams.'

AN ancient dream has wandered
 Through earth since the earliest time,
And he o'er whom it sweepeth
Grows stern—or it may be weepeth,
Like one who suffers with longing
 For a sweet yet terrible crime.

It hath but a single picture:
 A fountain which leaps and foams,
And by it a woman sits yearning,
Starting 'mid reveries—burning
 For a love which never comes.

The fountain leaps up in passion,
 Darts out in a gleaming pain;
And the longing of him who dreameth,
And the passion of her who seemeth,
 Fall back into foam again.

THE WORLD AND THE WORLD.

IF all the world must see the world
  As the world the world hath seen,
Then it were better for the world
  That the world had never been.

Yet if the world could see the world
  As the world the world might see,
Then a happier world than this old world
  Perhaps could never be.

Oh, world that lives upon the world !
  You travel far too slow !
Oh world ! green grave of all the world,
  How wondrous swift you go.

BUZZ!

'My name,' quoth the man, 'is Fine Ear; I can hear all the noises in the world, and all that is spoken therein.'—*Grimm's Fairy Tales.*

I HEARD the steeples pouring forth
  Their storm-bells' roaring din,
And the songs of merry companies
  As they sat so snug within;
The measured tread of armies proud,
  The dash of the restless sea,
'And it's buzz!' quoth the world, as on she whirled;
  And away with the world went we.

I heard a martyr at the stake
  Groan out, 'In Domino!'
I heard five infants squall at night,
  While cats yelled out below;
I heard a preacher pounding texts
  To a godly companie,
'And it's buzz!' quoth the world, as on she whirled;
  And away with the world went we.

I heard a dainty cavalier
  Sing to his ladye love,
While fountains in the moon-rays plashed,
  And the lady sighed above;

And I heard the click of cold white dice
  With curses pealing free,
'And it's buzz!' quoth the world, as on she whirled,
  And away with the world went we.

I heard a swan's sweet dying song,
  I heard the tempest's breath;
I heard a lady thrash her lord
  (And she thrashed him half to death);
I heard a scholar turning leaves;
  The scream of an angry flea.
'And its buzz!' quoth the world, as on she whirled;
  And away with the world went we.

Yes—music, thunder, growls, and groans,
  With shouts and shots in store,
While powder-mills exploded fast—
  But I could bear no more.
I stopped my ears—I howled a prayer,
  And swooned in agony,
'And it's buzz!' quoth the world, as on she whirled;
  And away with the world went we.

THE ROMAN RING.

I SAW you first upon a gem set in a Roman ring,
And I burned for it with longing as for a living thing.
The Greek who sees his heart's own love sold in a
 Turkish mart
Is not more grieved to think his purse is smaller than
 his heart,
Than I with many wishes and ducats very few
Was grieved to leave that lovely face behind me with
 the Jew.

Again I met you ripening and kindling into life
Beneath a skilful painter's brush as Vulcan's lovely
 wife,
From the foam and flood of colour, out-blushing
 lusciously,
As Venus Aphrodite rose from the summer sea;
And I waited with the patience of one whom fate en-
 twines,
And sees a new strange destiny around him spin its
 lines.

With doubting curiosity I watched the painter's face,
Yet earnestly and half in fear, to see if I could trace
A knowledge of the secret hope awaking with his art,
And how each crimson pencil-touch made blood leap
 in my heart.
In vain—for as he painted on, the likeness passed
 away,
And the rosy morning ended in a grim and cloudy day.

I meet you now in mortal form—a lovely living thing,
Still fairer than the vanished sketch, as that surpassed the ring,
And with new light the solemn text comes often to my mind,
That he who seeks right earnestly at last shall surely find.
Let others swear they find you fair and still fresh incense bring:
They did not know you, love, of old, upon the Roman ring.

THE FALL OF THE TREES.

I HAVE been in the wild green wilderness,
A wood of many ages, leagues away
From human home, when a tremendous storm
Was giving its long warning in those signs
Which every woodsman knows. We sat in peace
In the canoe dug from a single tree,
Well in the water and far out from shore,
For none at such a time will trust to trees,
Since lightning strikes them when they shelter men;
And as we sat and watched the wide-spread clouds,
I heard from time to time, long miles away,
Deep dull and thundering sounds, like cannon fired
In a ravine, which makes them heavier
And yet prolongs the roar. An awful sound
To one who knew that no artillery
Was in those lonely dales, and that no flash
Had shot as yet from heaven. It was the noise
Of ancient trees falling while all was still
Before the storm, in the long interval
Between the gathering clouds and that light breeze
Which Germans call the Wind's bride. At such time
The oldest trees go down, no one knows why,
But well I know from wood-experience
That 'tis before the storm they mostly fall,
And not while wind and rain are terrible.
'Tis wonderful, and seen ere every storm:—
Our great old statesmen died before the war.

THELEMÉ.

'Give me leave,' said Friar John, 'to found an abbey after my own fancy.' And Garagantua, well pleased, offered him all the country of Thelemé.—*Rabelais*, Book i. C. lvii.

I SAT one night on a palace step
  Wrapped up in a mantle thin,
And I gazed with a smile on the world without,
  With a growl at my world within.
Till I heard the merry voices ring
  Of a lordly companie,
And straight to myself I began to sing:
  'It is there I ought to be.'

And long I gazed through a lattice raised,
  Which looked from the old grey wall,
And my glance went in with the evening breeze,
  And ran o'er the revellers all.
And I said: 'If they saw me 'twould cool their mirth
  Far more than this wild breeze free;
But a merrier party was ne'er on earth,
  And among them I ought to be.'

And, oh, but they all were beautiful,
  Fairer than fairy dreams,
And their words were sweet as the wind-harp's tone
  When it sings o'er summer streams;

And they pledged each other with noble mien,
'True heart, with my life to thee!'
'Alack!' quoth I, 'but my soul is dry,
And among them I fain would be.'

And the gentlemen were noble souls,
Good fellows both sain and sound:
I had not deemed that a band like this
Could over the world be found;
And they spoke of brave and beautiful things,
Of all that was dear to me;
So I thought, 'Perhaps they would like me well
If among them I once might be!'

And lovely were the ladies too
Who sat in the lighted hall,
And one there was, oh, dream of life!
The loveliest of them all;
She sat alone by an empty chair,
The Queen of the feast was she;
And I said to myself, 'By that lady fair
I certainly ought to be!'

And aloud she spoke: 'We have waited long
For one who in fear and doubt
Looks wistfully into our Hall of Song,
As he sits on the steps without;
I have sung to him long in silent dreams,
I have led him o'er land and sea:
Go, welcome him in as his rank beseems,
And give him a place by me!'

They opened the door, yet I shrunk with shame
As I sat in my mantle thin,
But they haled me out with a joyous shout,
And merrily led me in,

And gave me a place by my bright-haired love
  As she wept with joy and glee,
So I said to myself: 'By the stars above,
  I am just where I ought to be!'

Farewell to thee, life of joy and grief!
  Farewell to thee, care and pain!
Farewell, thou cruel and selfish world,
  For I never will know thee again!
I live in a land where good fellows abound,—
  In Thelemé by the sea;
They may long for a happier life that will,—
  I am just where I ought to be.

THE RIDDLER.

THERE went a rider on a roan,
By rock and hill and all alone,
And asked of men these questions three:
'Who may the greatest miller be?
'What baker baked ere Adam's birth?
'And what washer washes the most on earth?'

And still the rider went his way
By cities old and castles gray,
In morning red or moonlight dim,
Unto the sea where ships do swim;
And yet no man could answer him.

He reined his horse upon the sand:
'There is no lord in any land
Can answer right my questions three:—
Old fisher sitting by the sea,
Can'st tell me where those craftsmen be?'

Then spoke the fisher of the mere:
'The earth is dark, the water clear,
And where the sea against the land
Is grinding rocks and shells to sand,
I see the greatest miller's hand.

'And the baker who baked ere the morn
When Adam was in Eden born,
Is Heat, that God made long before,
Which dries the sand upon the shore,
And hardens it to rock once more.

'And the water falling night and day
Is the washer, washing all away ;
All melts in time before the rain,
The mountain sinks into the plain :
So the great world comes and goes again.'

'Thou, Silver Beard, hast spoken well,
With wisdom most commendable ;
So bind thee with this golden band ! '
The light was red upon the strand,
The rider's road lay dark in-land.

MAIDEN'S LOVE.

THE fleetest horse in all the land,
So swift you cannot ride
But that his shadow on the sand
Will follow by your side.
And if your heart with love be sore
For one who feels your pain,
You cannot love that maiden more
Than she will love again.

So red a rosebud never blew
When opened by the wind,
But that one more as bright of hue
By seeking you may find.
And all that wooing lips e'er swore
Of greater truth is vain;
You cannot love a maiden more
Than she will love again.

The fairest fish upon the line
So matchless may not be,
But that some other fish as fine
Is swimming in the sea.
And love as man ne'er loved before,
This truth will still be plain;
You cannot love a maiden more
Than she will love again.

The horse will live while grass is free,
  The rose while wet with dew,
The fish while swimming in the sea,
  And love while love is true.
While light is in the sun above,
  And flowers are on the plain,
So long as you are true to love,
  She'll love you back again.

THE FOUNTAIN FAY.

YE gentles all who love your life
Beware, beware the water wife!

She singeth soft, she singeth low;
Her lute is the mountain-streamlet's flow;

Her harp the pine-wood's mournful moan;
She sits in the forest and sings alone,

And her songs like rippling rivers roll;
Beware, beware ere they drown thy soul!

Ride where you may, ride where you will,
The Fountain Fay may meet you still.

He rode alone in the silent night,
She swam like a star to his left and right.

He rode by the linden blooming fair,
The wood-bird sung: 'Oh, boy, beware!'

He came to the fountain in the wood;
The Fay in her beauty before him stood.

In the starlight, silver-sparkling glance
Her sisters swam in the Elfin dance.

'Alight, young minstrel, brave and gay,
And sing us thy sweetest, strangest lay!'

He tuned his lute, and the tinkling sounds
Flitted like birds through the greenwood bounds.

He sang so sweet—he sang so long,
The flower-buds opened to hear his song.

He sang so gently of maiden love,
He ripened the fruit on the boughs above.

'Far in the East is a rosy light.
What shall he have for his song this night?'

'I ask no more for lute and lay,
Than a kiss from the lips of the Fountain Fay!'

She kissed him once—to the minstrel's sight
The world seemed melting in golden light.

Once more, and his soul to the land of the fay
In beauty and music seemed floating away.

As she kissed him again the spirit had fled:
He lay in the moon-rays cold and dead.

But far from above a whisper fell:
'Green Earth, with thy valleys and lakes—farewell!'

Ye who know not the life of poësy,
Of beauty, romance, and fantasie!

And who think there can be 'no world like this,'
Beware of the Fairy—beware her kiss.'

A SPARK IN THE ASHES.

I WENT to a gay reception
  Last winter in the West,
As the beau of the belle of the season,
  Quite out of the season dressed.

For they told her no queen in story
  Had a bust so blanche and fair ;
And, like Samson, her strength and glory
  Was all in her wondrous hair.

But I did not think of her tresses,
  For directly vis-à-vis,
A dame in the simplest of dresses
  Was flashing her eyes at me.

Eternal eyes of wonder !
  How gloriously they rolled,
Like two black storm-lakes under
  An autumn forest of gold.

For as Lilith's in her splendour
  Like an aureole gleamed *her* head,
And a magic, strange yet tender,
  Seemed winding in every thread.

Wavy and dreamy in motion
  I felt the old memory flow :—
We had met by the sun-gold ocean
  A thousand years ago !

And the beaux and the belles with their graces,
  Where were *they* on the ancient shore?
Oh, the sea had blown froth in our faces
  A thousand years before.

Sea-foam and weed and clam-shells
  Which slid in the waves' long rolls!
Gay gentlemen—beautiful damsels!
  Why, how did you come by those souls?

THE TREES OF LIFE.

THE city belles in Autumn
  Their gayest garments don ;
In Autumn, too, the forests
  Put brighter vesture on.

At night in snowy linen
  The ladies sink to sleep ;
In winter 'neath the snow-drifts
  The trees seem slumbering deep.

Oh ! loves and leaves—among you
  A man must walk with care ;
How soon we're lost in forests !
  How soon 'mong ladies fair !

THE TWO FRIENDS.

I HAVE two friends—two glorious friends—two
better could not be,
And every night when midnight tolls they meet to
laugh with me.
The first was shot by Carlist thieves—ten years ago
in Spain.
The second drowned near Alicante—while I alive
remain.
I love to see their dim white forms come floating
through the night,
And grieve to see them fade away in early morning
light.
The first with gnomes in the Under Land is leading a
lordly life,
The second has married a mer-maiden, a beautiful
water-wife.
And since I have friends in the Earth and Sea—with
a few, I trust, on high,
'Tis a matter of small account to me—the way that I
may die.
For whether I sink in the foaming flood, or swing on
the triple tree,
Or die in my bed, as a Christian should, is all the
same to me.

IN THE OLD TIME.

WHAT is a Kiss?—pray tell't to Mee.
A daring daintie Fantasie:
A Brace of Birdes whych chirpe, 'wee would!'
And pyping answer: 'iff wee could!'

What is a Kiss?—when Evenyng falls
In russett Folds are Heaven's Walls,
Itt is a blissed Prophesye,
That Love wyll live, tho' Day may dye.

What is a Kiss?—when Mornyng's Leme
Casts Verjuice redd in Heaven's whyte Creme,
Itt is a pretie, ringing Knell,
That cryes to Love—'Swete, fare ye wel!'

What is a Kiss? Alacke! at worst,
A single Dropp to quenche a Thirst,
Tho' oft it prooves in happie Hour,
The first swete Dropp of one long Showre.

BRAVE HEART.

AFAR in the forest,
  Or deep in the town ;—
Where the sun rays come up,
  Or the wild waves go down ;
'Mid armies triumphant,
  In deserts alone,
While morning red gleameth,
  Brave Heart holds his own.

When true love sings sweetly,
  And white arms hold fast,
Or when love goes whistling
  Away with the blast ;
In kisses and music,
  By hatred's grim tone,
In rags or in ermine,
  Brave Heart holds his own.

When hunter's horn soundeth
  O'er river and rocks
Each soul with joy boundeth,
  In chasing the fox ;
And though the fox 'scape them
  Still pleasure they've known,
So through this world's hunting
  Brave Heart holds his own.

Love, fame, and a fortune
  May come or may go ;
Hate, Vengeance, and Murder,
  With all the mad show :—
But 'mid joys he hath garnered
  Or griefs he hath sown,
O'er his feelings and sorrows
  Brave Heart holds his own.

As the wild eagle saileth
  O'er sunshine and cloud,
As the dead nothing heareth
  Far down in his shroud,
As the tall man when bearded
  Hath child-dreams outgrown,
So through all this world's wearing
  Brave Heart holds his own.

GENTLE HEART.

'Vaut mieux être gentil que beau.'—*Romance de Griselidis.*

I KNOW that Beauty's power is great
  To lead to love the heedless mind;
That brilliant eyes may flit like stars,
  Yet leave an influence behind;
That lips, like ruby amulets,
  Oft hold unwilling souls in thrall;
Their spells are numberless—and yet
  A gentle heart is worth them all.

I know that Wit can lightly win
  What earthly charms have never won;
That Beauty fades before her light
  As moonlight pales before the sun;
That words enchant like elfin darts
  Although invisibly they fall,
And yet—though thousands own their might—
  A gentle heart is worth them all.

I know that Wealth can purchase Love:
  The best on earth are bought with gold;
That Power needs but to nod his head
  To win a myriad to his fold.
All these in turn must cling to Rank,
  Like grape-vines to the sunny wall:
The world is swayed by them, and yet
  A gentle heart is worth them all.

Sweet Dames, remember when ye strive
 To hold a lover in your thrall,
Wit, Beauty, Wealth, and Power may aid—
 A gentle heart is worth them all.

THE BRIDGE AND THE BROOK.

HE casts his arms around her,
But ever finds her gone ;
The love-span hath not bound her,
And still the brook runs on.

'Fair Sun! be thou, my dearest!'
She rose, his love to gain,
In dreamy, misty beauty,
But sunk in storm and rain.

Leave not for one above thee
Another tried for years :
A few brief hours he'll love thee,
Then cast thee back in tears.

MINE OWN.

AND oh, the longing, burning eyes !
  And oh, the gleaming hair
Which waves around me, night and day,
  O'er chamber, hall, and stair !

And oh, the step, half dreamt, half heard !
  And oh, the laughter low !
And memories of merriment
  Which faded long ago !

Oh, art thou Sylph—or truly Self—
  Or either at thy choice ?
Oh, speak in breeze or beating heart,
  But let me hear thy voice.

'Oh, some do call me Laughter, love ;
  And some do call me Sin :—'
'And they may call thee what they will
  So I thy love may win.

'And some do call me Wantonness,
  And some do call me Wine :—'
'Oh, they might call thee what they would
  If thou wert only mine !'

'And some do call me Sorrow, love,
  And some do call me Tears,
When sighing for the golden hours
  Of love in early years.

'And some do call me Gentle Heart,
  And some Forgetfulness:—'
'And if thou com'st as one or all,
  Thou comest but to bless!'

'And some do call me Life, sweetheart,
  And some do call me Death;
And he to whom the two are one
  Has won my heart and faith.'

She twined her white arms round his neck:—
  The tears fell down like rain.
'And if I live or if I die,
  We'll never part again.'

WOMAN'S WILL.

Con la muger y el dinero
No te burles, companero.

MANY a charm is round thee,
Many a spell hath bound thee,
Though awhile I give thee leave to range.
Soon, thy wild flight over,
Sóon, no more a rover,
Back thou'lt fly and never dare to change.
If thou wilt, go flutter
Here and there, to utter
Burning words to all with wanton will;
But—thou canst not leave me,
No—nor once deceive me;
And in chains I hold thee captive still.

To some love enchanting,
Every favour granting,
Go and sigh—I bid thee!—'tis in vain;
For no woman clever
Lost a lover ever
When she willed to hold him in her chain.
She who's sure of winning,
When the game's beginning
Throws away of course a stake or two;
But when higher aiming,
Bent on bolder gaming—
Back they come, and then she holds them true.

PORTRAITS.

LOUISE IN NORMANDY.

WE walked where storks and swallows fly,
Louise! Louise!
All on the castle-terrace high,
We saw the village in the sun,
We saw the sparkling waters run;
Birds fluttering, hearts a-beating.

Around your waist I twined my arm,
Louise! Louise!
I felt your life throb wild and warm;
But Love soon hushed the first alarm:
Birds fluttering, hearts a-beating.

We saw the peasants churchward climb,
Louise! Louise!
We heard the bells ring slow in chime,
And as they rung we kissed in time:
Birds fluttering, hearts a-beating.

Too slow the church-bells' melody!
Louise! Louise!
Yes; much too slow for you and me,
High over all where none could see:
Birds fluttering, hearts a-beating.

EVA.

I'VE seen bright eyes like mountain lakes,
  Reflecting heaven's blue ;
And some like black volcano-gulfs,
  With wildfire flashing through ;

But thine are like the eternal skies,
  Which draw the soul afar—
Their every glance a meteor,
  And every thought a star.

Some lips when robbed seem cherries sweet,
  —Small sin to those who stole—
But thine are like the Eden fruit,
  Whose theft may cost a soul.

Oh, coral fruit of Paradise !
  Who would not grasp the prize ?
With heaven so near to bring him back,
  In those eternal eyes.

MANUELA.

RED the lips of Manuela—
How the lady loves to kiss!

Ah, when Manuela kisses,
First she kisses with her glances!
Then her red lips kiss each other,
Practising for warm encounters.

Then she kisses with her eyelids,
Kisses with her arching eyebrows,
With her soft cheek softly rubbing,
With her chin and hands and fingers.

All the frame of Manuela,
All her blood and all her spirit,
All melt down to burning kisses:
All she feeds on is their sugar.

Oh, thou sun above us flying!
Breeze from land to land still roaming,
Saw ye ever yet a lady
Half so fair or fond of kissing?

Red the lips of Manuela—
How the lady loves to kiss!

ERMENGILDE.

FAR in the forest
  'Mid the rocks,
His hands unwound
  Her heavy locks.
In the tawny waves
  They swam with bliss,
While red lips pressed
  The close wet kiss.
Oh, broken leaves and withered flowers,
Ye witnesses of golden hours !
Spring up afresh, and tell to none
Why your white sides are towards the sun.

Beneath the vines,
  Where none could hear,
Vines seem too human
  Creeping near ;
Awed with their secret
  Dread-confessed,
Yet both half-lost
  In being bless'd.
Oh, river swimming to the sea,
Our death-pall thou shouldst quickly be,
If one in all the world could dream
That we had kissed beside thy stream.

CALLIRHOE.

DARK eyes—dark eyes—pale, earnest face,
  Oh, when I feel your power,
The world seems mean and pitiful,
  Its fiercest storm a shower.

Dark eyes—eternal soul of pride!
  Deep life of all that's true!
Oh, what were death or anything
  To one full thought of you?

Away, away to other skies!
  Away o'er sea and sands!
Such eyes as those were never made
  To shine in earthly lands.

MIRIAM.

OH Miriam! Pearl of the morning, gazelle of the palm-land, soul of my spirit,
Daughter of Akiba, beloved of the faithful and the Goyim!
Blue sea; sister of lilies and roses!
There came to me a dream fresh on the wings of the morning,
Soft as the light of the Silver Sabbath lamp, when it shines on the Pesach feast.
Dear as thine eye when loveliest beaming, love's sister.
I walked by thy side in a dream; we walked by a river:—
Jordan rolls not more gently: purple its waters;
Thine eyes were upon me, beloved, thy star-light eyes, blessed as the lamp of the Sanctuary,
Black eyes of infinite fire—oh soul, thou art lovely!
Beauty of the East—the golden sequins and ear-rings—the antique gold of Judea,
Which hangs upon thy forehead with the golden ear-rings from Damascus,
Which thou had'st from Sara thy aunt—all the gold around thy dear face
Is but the frame of a picture too fine for its setting,
My arm and thine twined like the vines in spring,

Slowly we walked and slower, till trembling and
pausing,
I kissed thee, oh beloved!—on the sand by the purple
waters.
Anna the gracious is fair; fair, too, is Sara the
mistress;
Abigail the joy of her father, and Ruth the satisfied;
Tabitha the roe-buck, light are her footsteps and
lovely;
Esther the secret and silent, and Rachel the sheep;
Eva life giving; Judith praising, confessing;
Jemima fair as the day; Hagar, the stranger;
Hannah gracious and merciful; Huldah all the
world;
Yes, all the world and its loveliness hath nothing like
thine, little sister!
Thy bitterness, oh Miriam, is sweeter than all their
sweetness!

FLORENCE.

THE winds still rock the merry waves,
And the blue waves shake the shore ;
But thine azure eyes and gentle words
Will move my heart no more.

Oh Sea ! thou may'st well be glorious
With thy snow-capped sapphire waves ;
There's a fairer white and a deeper blue
Deep hid in thy silent caves.

Oh Wind ! thou may'st well be wailing
With thy moaning, droning sound,
For a sweeter, softer voice than thine
By the wind in the water drowned.

Oh Sea and Wind !—together,
Since first your course has run,
Ye have ta'en the brave and beautiful :—
Could ye not spare us *one ?*

Not *one !*—in the breezy morning
Thou'lt wake me no more from dreams :
Not *one !*—in the dewy evening
I shall miss thine eyes' blue gleams.

THEN AND NOW.

WE met and spoke in darkness,
  But my spirit knew your grace,
And my heart had felt your fetters
  Ere my eyes had seen your face.

That evening dream is over,
  No cloud between us rolls ;
Now the light is on our faces,
  And the darkness in our souls.

THE PROPHET.

THE prophet said: 'All mysteries
  Unto me are displayed,
Yet not the Eagle's way in air
  Or a man's who woos a maid!

Then I said to myself, 'I soon will solve
  This subtle mystery;'
So I asked the man and the maid, but they
  Knew even less than he.

A SONG WITHOUT AN END.

THE crow in the woods is cawing
  A solemn Indian rhyme,
And the cat-bird cries while the wood-pecker
  Is merrily beating time;

The leaves are sweetly rustling
  As the west wind sweeps along;
Yet all is but the symphony
  Of a deeper and stranger song.

And when bird and leaf are silent,
  And quiet my spirit wins,
Then first with wondrous melody
  The Song of the Wood begins.

WAKING DREAMS.

THAT thought is no reality,
  Oft waking with a start, we find ;
But from reality take thought,—
  How little then remains behind.

I walk the greenwood all alone,
  And thou in spirit by my side ;
Ah, then thou art indeed my own,
  A something more than earthly bride.

A dead leaf falls, the vision flies
  Like morning mist from mountain stream,—
Yet take that vision from my life,
  And life itself were but a dream !

MOUNTAIN AND SEA.

WHEN gazing on a summer sea
  Beneath a purple sky,
It oft has seemed a mountain ridge
  Far rising blue and high.

Now gazing inland and afar,
  The thought still comes to me,
How much yon distant mountain line
  Is like the dim blue sea.

When thou art seated by my side
  Loved memories ever rise;
When thou art gone up swells the tide
  Of those sweet, sea-blue eyes.

WHERE ?

DEEP in the dale the gold veins hide,
Far up ascends the mountain's brow ;
But soul of gold and front of pride,
Where in this wide world bidest thou?

Night blesses me. The heart grows sweet
In silence 'neath dark violet skies ;
But where are now her fairy feet ?
And whose and where her starry eyes ?

Soul of the Eagle! If I knew
That thou but tread'st life soil or sands !
Life of the mountain torrents—who
Hath heard thee sing in silent lands ?

Unbounded one! could I but feel
Thou liv'st,—though in the Infinite,—
How calmly unto thee I'd kneel,
And worship in the perfumed night!

Moon Queen and Love Star ! ye behold
All tender mysteries—all things fair—
From the dim rites of Sidon old
Through all Earth's beauty—was she there ?

Proud serpent-beauty—Crested Queen!
  The tenderest dream this heart has known,
Art thou to be or hast thou been
  My life—my death—my golden One!

Yes, while the rivers laughing run
  To meet in love the foaming sea,
While flowers grow fragrant 'neath the sun,
  I know from them that thou must be.

I know where miners seek their gold,
  Where Heaven kiss the mountain's brow;
But, soul of beauty—pride untold—
  Where in this wide world hidest thou?

EUTHANASIA.

I WOKE at water dashing:
  At my window, bright as stars,
Two dark brown eyes were flashing
  Their love light through the bars.

'Thou cam'st to me in spirit
  Amid our mountain streams;—
Now thou shalt woo me waking,
  As once thou did'st in dreams.'

And forth once more in darkness
  Twin souls have flown afar;
Lo, yonder in the land of light,
  There shines another star.

FROST PICTURES.

I.

WINTER came on, and the frost went down
O'er field and forest and flood and town.

It found the windows clear at night ;
But when morning came, with its golden light,

They were all like silver, fair to see,
Chased in wonderful imagery.

'A New Year's gift to the world!' said the frost,
Rich lace curtains which nothing cost.'

And over the wide world he went his way,
Till he passed a cell where a prisoner lay.

Then he worked the windows thickly and white,
And went freezing, freezing—on through the night.

The prisoner woke ere morning grey,
And saw that the frost had been that way,

Then he wrote on the silvery crispy rind
The thought that ever was on his mind :

'O cara mî Jesu, nunc libera me!'
(Dear Lord, from this prison pray set me free!)

Then lighted his taper, and all alone
Read in the silence till morning shone.

The Lord in the Castle sleepless lay ;
Long were the hours, and he wished for day,

When all at once on his chamber wall
He saw these letters bright-flickering fall :

'O cara mî Jesu, nunc libera me !'
(Dear Lord, from this prison pray set me free !)

Borne through the night from the prison cell,
The frost and the taper had carried them well.

Upstarted the lord, amazed I ween,
For a stranger sight he had never seen.

And sought till he found what the cause might be,
And then set the prisoner fairly free,

Who had writ on his window unthinkingly,
'O cara mî Jesu, nunc libera me !'

II.

THE frost upon the window
  Has painted all in ice,
Castles and caverns and crystals
  With many a wild device.

And with my breath it painted ;
  But soon in the morning ray
The castle and caverns and crystals
  Went running to nothing away.

The frost made wondrous pictures
  With breath, and all in fun,
Just as full many a speaker
  More seriously has done.

Building up domes in figures,
  Painting in metaphor rare,
Making with breath his pictures,
  Frosty and chilling and fair.

But when some great genial spirit
  Came forth with a heart-warmed ray,
The frosty and crystalline figures
  To nothing went fading away.

'PERSEVERANDO.'

STILL firm in purpose ever be,
  Wherever drifts the tide,
And bear in mind, whate'er we see,
  The world to all is wide.

Still firm in purpose ever be ;
  The soaring albatross
Sometimes must land on barren sand,
  'Mid withered weeds and moss :
Sometimes be lower than the gulls, —
  Crawl lower than the sea ;
But when he once can spread his wings,
  Far, far away goes he.

Great albatross !—the meanest birds
  Spring up and flit away,
While thou must toil to gain a flight,
  And spread those pinions grey ;
But when they once are fairly poised,
  Far o'er each chirping thing
Thou sailest wide to other lands,
  E'en sleeping on the wing.*

* Many sea-birds find it difficult to rise from the ground, and are obliged to run a few paces or struggle before they can fly.

Oh ! heart, hold fast, though hard it be
  At first to win the way ;
The darkest morning in the end
  May prove the brightest day ;
As weak a boat has reached the port,
  In spite of every tide :—
Fear not that every course will fail
  Until the whole are tried.

AMERICA AND COLUMBIA.

THROUGH years of toil Columbus
  Unto our New World came;
But a charlatan skipped after,
  And gave that world his name.

All day in street and market
  The liar's name we see;
Columbia!—sweet and seldom—
  Is left to Poetry.

And the names bring back a lesson
  Taught to the world in youth—
That the realm of Song and Beauty
  Is the only home of Truth.

SPRING.

UPROSE the wild old winter-king,
And shook his beard of snow ;
'I hear the first young hare-bell ring,
'Tis time for me to go!
Northward o'er the icy rocks,
Northward o'er the sea,
My daughter comes with sunny locks:
This land's too warm for me!'

And softly came the fair young queen
O'er mountain, dale, and dell;
And where her golden light was seen
An emerald shadow fell.
The good-wife oped the window wide,
The good-man spanned his plough;
''Tis time to run, 'tis time to ride,
For Spring is with us now.'

And the city-maiden smiled that day
In all her loveliness ;
'I must pack my furs and things away,
And think of a new spring dress,
A new chapeau—a feather fine,
Light gloves, and ribbons gay.'
Oh, winter wild!—oh, maiden mine,
Thus runs the world away.

THE LANGUAGE OF THE SEA.

I SPOKE—but if my voice was heard,
  You did not answer me,
But looked with painful earnestness
  Far at the foaming sea.

The breakers caught the glance and thought,
  And in a wondrous strain,
With tones of solemn melody
  They brought them back again.

And what your glances did not tell
  I heard in that deep voice,
And what to you was strange and sad
  First made my heart rejoice.

Oh, it was well that none around
  Who laughed so merrily,
Had ever learned on life's great shore
  The language of the sea.

LONG AGO.

MANY a weary year
  Since I waltzed, my love, with thee !
And neither of us knows
  Where the other one may be ;
Dying in iron sorrow,
  Or sunk in the endless sea.

Many a quiet year
  Since those wild old nights ran by—
Mornings in the forest,
  Days on the mountains high,
Galleries of golden art :—
Enough, enough, thou beating heart—
  I would not have thee die !

Galleries of golden art,
  And music soft and low,
And friends in youth—oh, now in truth
  Some faint relief I know.
And is she dead ?—hurrah, my heart !
  Here comes the hot tears' flow !

LOST DREAMS.

VOICES, voices ever round me crying!
  Voices in the midnight in the storm!
Voices deep in slumber softly sighing!
  Memories which long ago lost form!
Memories which once too lightly faded
  Out of life, and *now* with endless pain
In such tone and colour darkly shaded,
  Strive in agony to live again.

Golden images of early morning!
  When I stood in youth beside a sea
Fringed with palaces, why did no warning
  Ring from ivory windows unto me?
Voices! had ye *then* but softly spoken—
  'Print these pictures ever on thy soul!'
Ye would not be wailing now and broken,
  Agonized with tasks beyond control.

By the sea and in the silent valleys,
  On the lakes where morning mists arise,
Or in gardens old, through flowery alleys,
  Still they live—those gleams of Paradise:
Dim, too dim, alas! for aught but feeling,
  Light,—too light for mind to hold them long;
Only now and then a form revealing,
  Summoned by the magic spell of SONG.

For the artist is the true magician!
  Form may die, but harmony still lives;
Death and Time may take away volition,
  Not the reflex which true beauty gives
To Art creative—and thus every poet
  Who brings soul-music forth with many a pain,
Like her of Endor, though he may not know it,
  To others shows the glorious dead again.

IN A DREAM.

AND thou shalt walk as in a dream,
Thine eyes bewildered by the gleam
Of blending light, till future years
Have chased thy present midnight fears.

And thou shalt walk as in a dream,
Yet oft through memory will it seem
That one who should have been a guide—
Or friend, is wanting by thy side.

And thou shalt walk as in a dream,
With nothing as it now doth seem;
Till all delusion pass away,
And thou'rt alone in brightest day.

For in thy heart thou bear'st the key
Which yet *must* set thy spirit free,
And lead thee to th' eternal stream :—
Though now thou walkest in a dream.

PARADISE LOST.

AND we are in the winter,
  Sadly chilled with frost and snow!
Oh, how strange amid my memories
  Seems last summer's rosy glow.

When your bright eyes opened on me
  Like two dew-filled lotus flowers,
When I saw myself reflected
  In the depths of Heaven's bowers.

But in my deepest rapture
  It all vanished—and I fell
Back to artificial roses :—
  Heavenly lotus, fare thee well!

THE DIFFERENCE.

CLOTILDA writes such glowing verses,
  Maria scarce with prose can play ;
Ah me! how oft an idle fancy
  Leads mortals from the narrow way.

For when it came to *real* singing
  Clotilda dared not hum a line,
While fair Maria, like a Sappho,
  Poured forth her soul in thrills divine.

HOW THE ENGINEER DIED AT DESJARDINS.'

The engineer (brave fellow) whistled "down brakes," and while endeavouring to avert the catastrophe went down with the engine. Instead of attempting to escape at the first warning, he staid until the moment when the engine was precipitated into the abyss, and was reversing it and endeavouring to prevent if possible the fatal results.'—*N. Y. Albany Evening Journal*, 1856.

THE locomotive screamed along,
  A darting death on wings;
And the smoke puffed out its masses black,
  As hell its legions flings,
Over the track, right down the road,
  Swift as the desert wind,
With a draw-bridge gaping wide before,
  And a hundred souls behind.

The engineer looked out, and saw
  That hope was all in vain,
Yet whistled to the brakesman—*down!*
  'I'll die, or save the train.'
And did he leap to save himself?
  No—in a desperate strife
He wrestled with the Iron Fiend,
  True to the last in life.

True to the heart, not caring though
  The last faint chance were gone,
While like a thundering avalanche
  The roaring train flew on,
Right o'er the draw—right down the gulf,
  In one tremendous fall.
'Mid screaming steam and crashing iron,
  Went engineer and all.

Man of the road !—May truth itself
  Judge well this thought of mine,
That I do deem it worth a life
  To die a death like thine !
The Roll of Honour will not end,
  Nor the Martyrs' list be done,
Till that Desjardins engineer
  Be written down as one.

SONGS OF THE

AMERICAN WAR OF EMANCIPATION,

1861—1865.

THE KNIGHT AND THE DRAGON.

JULY, 1861.

WHEN I wandered in the land of Art
'Mid the sharp-tipped dreams, where blue Madonnas
Sit like butterflies upon a sunflower,
Framed in fragments of the Golden Ages,
Oft I noted that in all Cathedrals,
Here or there amid grotesquest carving,
One quaint symbol never was forgotten–
Soon or later I was sure to find it
Lurking somewhere in entrellised columns ;
Peeping strangely through a gnarling impost,
Always came the strange Masonic symbol
Of a warrior, helmeted and sworded,
Fighting grimly with a devil dragon.

Good old priests have told me that the figure
Simply meant St George :—you know the story—
Deeper heads will have it 'tis a symbol,
Persian-old—the myth of Light and Darkness,
Ahriman and Ormuzd fiercely fighting,
Ever fighting the great world-old battle.

And it is the fight of Light and Darkness,
The great fight of God against the Devil :
The great fight of Tyranny and Freedom ;
Truth and Right against foul Might and Falsehood :
Many a thousand years the two have battled—
Tell me, is it an unending struggle ?

Many voices cry, 'It is unending;
Man is damned by birth, for black transgression
And the lust of power are his nature,
Slavery, like sin, must last for ever:
Woe unto the weaker—woe eternal;
God and Sin and Pain have plainly spoken,
And the Earth will ne'er be free from bondage.'

Let me see once more that ancient carving:
No; it is not a mere balanced battle;
True, the knight seems smothered by the dragon,
True, the foul and snaky folds are round him;
True, he gasps amid the flame and poison;
But his blade is in the monster's vitals,
And the grisly drake is slowly dying.

Yes, although so slowly, he *is* dying;
Many thousand years have fled in darkness
Since the sword first cut his scaly armour,
And the red wound roused him into madness;
But the good knight is of race immortal—
Ever young, and passionate, and fearless;
And the strength which oozes from the dragon
Blooms reviving in the glorious warrior.

Ancient dragon, you are slowly dying!
Golden warrior, ever fairer, stronger!
Child of Light, my great Prometheus-Balder,
Dear and beautiful and never-fading,
Rouse! for now the fire-drake makes him ready
For his maddest, fiercest, foulest struggle—
Rouse!

Oh, countrymen! men of the Northland
All around you twines the Southern dragon,
All your life is blent with subtle poison,
All your veins are fired with heat infernal,

From the loathsome devil's spume and breathing:
Strike, my warrior, strike him dead for ever!
End the world-old strife between the oppressor
And the oppressed: press on, for you *must* conquer.

Now the good knight frees him from the dragon,
Casts aside the ancient heavy armour,
Bathes him in the purest light of heaven,
In the intensest lucent-flowing spirit;
White and beautiful and lithe and naked,
Oh! how golden fair withouten armour!
True, it shielded him for many ages;
True, it guarded him against the dragon;
But it always was a heavy armour,
Girding, smothering, chafing unto bleeding
Those fair limbs of ivory-purest beauty:
Strange that thousands should have dreamed that armour
Was his chiefest charm and best worth keeping;—
Soul of Beauty;—rule this world for ever.

A SONG OF '62.

THERE'S a sorrowful old story how the army of the Turk
Once fell into an ambush, full of blood and evil work;
When the fate-believing Moslem, caring not that all was gone,
With sword a-sheath and eyes firm closed right into death rode on.

He could not fly—his hour had come—and so he kissed the rod
With La il Allah! on his lips, gave all the rest to God:
Down rolled the rocks—the muskets roared—in heaps the Faithful fell,
But one escaped of all the host the dreadful tale to tell.

But there's another story, how a slave, in cruel sport,
Was thrown unto a tiger before the Roman court.
The man was born of fighting blood, and so he turned at bay:
The Roman at the tiger!—and the great brute slunk away!

Hurrah! we're called to battle—hurrah! the word is
'fight!'
We've a bloody day before us, perhaps a deathly
night.
But let there happen what there may in all our battle-
work,
We'll pattern by the Roman, and never by the Turk.

CAVALRY SONG.

1862.

WEAPONED well to war we ride,
With sabres ringing by our side,
The warning knell of death to all,
Who hold the holiest cause in thrall,
The sacred Right
Which grows to Might,
The day which dawns in blood-red light.

Weaponed well to war we ride,
To conquer, tide what may betide,
Since never yet beneath the sun
Was battle by the devil won;
For what to thee
Defeat may be
Time makes a glorious victory.

Weaponed well to war we ride—
Who braves the battle wins the bride;
Who dies the death for truth shall be
Alive in love eternally.
Though dead he lies,
Soft starry eyes
Smile hope to him from purple skies.

Weaponed well to war we ride:—
Hurrah for the surging thunder-tide!
When the cannon's roar makes all seem large,
And the war-horse screams in the crashing charge,
        And the rider strong
        Whom he bears along
Is a death-dart shot at the yielding throng.

Weaponed well to war we ride:
The ball is open, the hall is wide;
The sabre as it quits the sheath,
And beams with the lurid light of death,
        And the deadly glance
        Of the glittering lance,
Are the taper-lights of the battle-dance.

Weaponed well to war we ride,
Find your foeman on either side;
But woe to those who miss the time
When one false step is a deadly crime:
        Who loses breath
        In the dance of death
Wins nor wears nor wants the wreath.

Weaponed well to war we ride—
Our swords are keen and our cause is tried;
When the sharp edge cuts and the blood runs free,
May we die in the hour of victory!
        We feel no dread—
        The battle bed,
Where'er it be, has heaven o'erhead.

THE PROCLAMATION.*

SEPTEMBER 22, 1862.

NOW who has done the greatest deed
  Which History has ever known?
And who in Freedom's direst need
  Became her bravest champion?
Who a whole continent set free?
  Who killed the curse and broke the ban
Which made a lie of liberty?
  You—Father Abraham—you're the man!

The deed is done. Millions have yearned
  To see the spear of freedom cast:—
The dragon writhed and roared and burned:
  You've smote him full and square at last.
O Great and True! *You* do not know,
  You cannot tell—you cannot feel
How far through time your name must go,
Honoured by all men, high or low,
  Wherever Freedom's votaries kneel.

* This poem was written on the day when the Proclamation appeared.

This wide world talks in many a tongue—
  This world boasts many a noble state—
In *all* your praises will be sung,
  In all the great will call you great.
Freedom ! Where'er that word is known,
  On silent shore, by sounding sea,
'Mid millions or in deserts lone,
  Your noble name shall ever be.

The word is out—the deed is done—
  The spear is cast—dread no delay.
When such a steed is fairly on
  Fate never fails to find a way.
Hurrah ! hurrah ! The track is clear,
  We know your policy and plan ;
We'll stand by you through every year :
  Now, Father Abraham, you're our man.

WHEN THE CAPTAIN IS READY TO RIDE.

FEBRUARY 17, 1863.

Air—'*Was helfen mir tausend Ducaten, tra la.*'

IN the morning when trumpets are sounding, *tra la,*
  Our horses are quickly untied,
And fast down the road we go bounding—*tra la,*
  Or over the meadow-land ride ;

CHORUS.

  For we are the boys of the sword,
  Who can jump from the bed or the board,
And be off like a shot to the skirmishing hot,
When the Captain is ready to ride.

'Well, scout, have you something to tell us ?'—*tra la,*
  'The rebels are hid by the hill,
And the fellows believe they can sell us—*ah ha !*
  But I know of a road by the mill.'

'We'll give them no chances to turn on the heel,
  We'll give them the powder and ball ;
We'll give them the bullet, we'll give them the steel ;
  We'll give them the devil and all !'

Hurrah for the battle! Hurrah for a bout!
How we scatter the soldiers of sin!
When our cavalry spreads like a thunder-cloud out,
And drives like a thunderbolt in.

Hurrah for the men of the sword!
Who fight for the cause of the Lord!
Oh, the sabre's sharp edge is the entering wedge
In a war to let liberty in.

THE BEGINNING OF THE END.

OCTOBER 27, 1864.

THAT I have lived to know this time,
  That I have lived this fight to see,
Through Slavery's night to Freedom's prime,
  Is Heaven's own holiest joy to me.
I do not ask to see the end,
  For what am I to be so blest?
Enough for me the strife's begun,
  And God will care for all the rest.
    Through blood-red clouds the light I see,
    Nunc dimittis Domine!

Gone are those nightmares of the past,
  The hardening fear—the lingering doubt,
If Lord or Slave unto the last
  Must be our parts to still act out.
How oft they came—those fiendish thoughts,
  Like vampires rising from the grave;
'Oh, call your labour what you will,
  The labourer is always slave.'
    From all devilish doubt set free,
    Nunc dimittis Domine!

The world has seen a thousand wars,
  To test humanity's great truth,
Yet still the prison kept its bars,
  And still the strife was one of youth,
Of headlong Youth with wary Age:
  But Man is somewhat wiser grown,
While Ancient Evil weakens fast,
  And soon it shall be overthrown.
    Saints have prayed this time to see,
    Nunc dimittis Domine!

And thus spoke God: 'Out of the North'
  (In every age the place of doom),
'Behold, great evil shall come forth.'
  Wail! South-land, wail!—for it has come.
'Woe to the South!'—the word went forth
  In solemn warning years ago,
And many on the border laughed:—
  The bolt is shot—now let it go!
    Lord! we bow our heads to thee!
    Nunc dimittis Domine!

Ho! Northmen of the stormy coast!
  Ye chosen with the avenging sword,
Called forth—it is no idle boast—
  To do the bidding of the Lord,
Go on! And this ye shall not lose,
  This to your name shall glory lend,
That Northmen in the world's long fight
  First brought the battle towards an end.
    'Tis the end of Slavery.
    Nunc dimittis Domine!

FREE !

1865.

FREE, free, free
The whole land shall be,
North and South, from sea to sea,
Free—for ever free !

Free, free, free
Shall all our labour be,
Without a lash, without a chain,
Without reproach, without a strain,
Without a sneer or rankling word,
Without a dungeon and the cord:—
North and South, from sea to sea,
Free—for ever free!

Free, free, free
Our Speech shall ever be ;
Far as Earth's waters run and ring,
Far as the wild birds soar or sing,
Where voice may speak and voice reply,
And white-winged sheets like angels fly,
North and South, from sea to sea,
Free—for ever free!

Free, free, free
Our Thought shall ever be,
Yes, freer yet with every year;
What man may dare or heart holds dear
Shall ring and roll through every land
In speech which all may understand.
North and South, from sea to sea,
Free—for ever free.

Free, free, free!
And God our guide shall be!
He led our fathers on of old
Through trials dark and manifold,
Till they the mark appointed won;
Us will he lead yet further on,
Till all shall be, from sea to sea,
Free—for ever free.

REAL INCIDENTS.

BLUE AND GREY.

DECEMBER, 1865.

I.

'THE only difference in your war,'
  I heard a stranger say,
'Is that one side is dressed in blue,
  The other clad in grey.'

I went into a Federal camp,
  I heard the soldiers cry:
'Hurrah! there come the newspapers!'
  And saw them rush to buy.

I went along the Valley Road,
  And met upon my way
Ten of Lee's straggling infantry,
  All dressed in rebel grey.

One held a proclamation out,
  And as I stopped my steed,
Said: 'Tell us what this paper says?
  For none of us can read!'

And I spoke out :—' If you could read,
  And find out what is true,
Instead of wearing Davis grey,
  You'd bear the Lincoln blue.'

Grey is the colour of the dust
  In which the serpent crawls,
And blue the hue of heaven, which looks
  Down on earth's prison walls.

II.

ONE day, when I was on the march,
  In Eighteen Sixty-three,
The very day when General Meade
  Was driving General Lee
Before him out of Maryland,
  With all his chivalry :

We passed a school-house on the road,
  The benches scattered round ;
But, ah! the scholars, where were they?
  For no familiar sound
Of lessons conned, or pleasant play,
  Was heard in all the bound.

I entered, and I stood alone ;
  The troop went slowly by,
And fainter grew the captain's tone,
  And faint the driver's cry ;
The heavy cannon's clank and groan
Still lessened, passing further on,
  Yet never seemed to die :—
Was it an echo all my own,
  Or the wild brook running nigh ?

I looked around, and on the walls
  I read in writing clear :
' *We've gained the day, we'll soon have all*
  The country far and near,'
Signed by a rebel officer,
  A boasting cavalier.

Hodie tibi, cras mihi,
  Beneath this vaunting strain,
'To-day is thine, to-morrow mine,'
  I wrote as clear and plain:
No doubt it pleased the schoolmaster
  When he came back again!

'Twixt Boonsboro' and Hagerstown
  That log-hut school-house stands,
The writing still upon the wall:
  But where are now the bands
Which swept so proudly up and down,
  O'er all the border lands?-
Oh! whither went the stately house
  Which stood upon the sands?

The foregoing incidents are from my own personal experience.—C. G. L.

THE END.

www.ingramcontent.com/pod-product-compliance
Lightning Source LLC
LaVergne TN
LVHW021200120826
845150LV00011B/1646

* 9 7 8 1 4 2 5 5 1 3 8 5 6 *